SILVER SCREENS

The Merrill lights up West Wisconsin Avenue on a July evening, 1924. Photo by Albert Kuhli

Silver Screens

A PICTORIAL HISTORY OF MILWAUKEE'S MOVIE THEATERS

LARRY WIDEN AND JUDI ANDERSON

WISCONSIN HISTORICAL SOCIETY PRESS

Published by the
Wisconsin Historical Society Press

www.wisconsinhistory.org

Photographs identified with PH, WHi, or WHS are from the Society's collections; address inquiries about such photos to the Visual Materials Archivist at the above address.

Publications of the Wisconsin Historical Society Press are available at quantity discounts for promotions, fund raising, and educational use. Write to the above address for more information.

Printed in the United States of America

Cover and interior designed by Jane Tenenbaum

Front cover photo by Albert Kuhli
Back cover photos: Allis/Dave Prentice Collection; Fern/Karl Thiede Collection; Rainbow/Karl Thiede Collection; Kosciuszko/Larry Widen Collection; Rivoli/Photo by Guy Brackett, Diane Morgan Collection; Riverside interior/Photo by Larry Widen

11 10 09 08 07   1 2 3 4 5

Portions of this text were originally published in *Milwaukee Movie Palaces,* © Milwaukee County Historical Society, 1986.

Library of Congress Cataloging-in-Publication Data

Widen, Larry.
  Silver screens : a pictorial history of Milwaukee's movie theaters / Larry Widen and Judi Anderson.
    p. cm.
  Revised ed. of Milwaukee movie palaces. © 1986.
  Includes bibliographical references and index.
  ISBN-13: 978-0-87020-368-8 (pbk. : alk. paper)
  ISBN-10: 0-87020-368-1 (pbk. : alk. paper)
  1. Motion picture theaters—Wisconsin—Milwaukee—Pictorial works. 2. Motion picture theaters—Wisconsin—Milwaukee. I. Anderson, Judi. II. Title.

PN1993.5.U814W55 2007
791.4309775'95—dc22

                                                                              2006010120

The activity that is the subject of this book has been financed in part with Federal funds from the National Park Service, U.S. Department of the Interior. However, the contents and opinions do not necessarily reflect the views or policies of the Department of the Interior.

This program receives Federal financial assistance for identification and protection of historic properties. Under Title VI of the Civil Rights Act of 1964, Section 504 of the Rehabilitation Act of 1973, and the Age Discrimination Act of 1975, as amended, the U.S. Department of the Interior prohibits discrimination on the basis of race, color, national origin, disability or age in its federally assisted programs. If you believe you have been discriminated against in any program, activity, or facility as described above, or if you desire further information, please write to: Office of Equal Opportunity, National Park Service, 1849 C Street, N.W., Washington, D.C. 20240.

♾ The paper used in this publication meets the minimum requirements of the American National Standard for Information Sciences-Permanence of Paper for Printed Library Materials, ANSI Z39.48-1992.

CONTENTS

Milwaukee Sentinel

ACKNOWLEDGMENTS

The Milwaukee County Historical Society published our book *Milwaukee Movie Palaces* in 1986. Compiling an accurate history for that book meant consulting hundreds of sources. Like detectives from an old *film noir*, we searched attics, basements, historical societies, former theater buildings, and libraries. We consulted hundreds of old newspapers, municipal records, city directories, insurance maps, tax rolls, and historic photographs. Not surprisingly, the single most valuable resource turned out to be personal interviews with the people who were part of Milwaukee's theater legacy.

Since then we have continued our research. Although it's been twenty years since *Milwaukee Movie Palaces* was published, many people have contacted us, offering corrections, new photos, illustrations, stories, and memoirs. *Silver Screens* is an expansion of *Milwaukee Movie Palaces* but by no means a reprint. Although it retains much of the history included in the first book, the original narrative has been rewritten to include new findings on drive-ins, projection booths, movie promotions, noted theater personalities, and much more. It also includes dozens of rare photos and illustrations that have never before been published.

We are grateful to the many people who have so generously assisted us along the way, and we wish to recognize them here. For allowing us to mine valuable information from their memories as part of an interview, thanks go to the late Harry Boesel, former Fox-Wisconsin and Marcus Theatres manager; Evelyn Conway, wife of the late theater manager Charles Conway; Don Goeldner, former theater projectionist; Mary Granberg, granddaughter of Thomas Saxe; Wally Konrad, retired theater manager; Robert Klein, retired Marcus Theatres executive; Connie Murphy, whose family owned the Airway and Avenue Theaters; Dave Prentice, for access to his historic photo collection; the late Joe Reynolds, for fifty years of theater stories; the late Catherine Saxe, daughter of Thomas Saxe; Truman Schroeder, retired Marcus Theatres executive; the late Milton Schultz, former theater employee; Neal Seegert, son of the owners of the Regent Theater; the late Harold Shaffer, an usher in the early days of the Tower; and the late Estelle Steinbach, a Fox-Wisconsin Theater manager.

For their help along the way, we thank Harry Anderson and Robert Teske, the former and current executive directors of the Milwaukee County Historical Society; Eric Levin, manager of the Times Theater; and Christel Maas, of the Golda Meir Library, UW–Milwaukee. Special thanks go to the late David Schwartz, preeminent Milwaukee bookseller, for his friendship and desire to see this work published.

For research assistance, thanks to Clayborn Benson, of the Wisconsin Black Historical Society and Museum; Steve Daily, of the Milwaukee County Historical Society; Thomas Eschweiler, of the Wisconsin Architectural Archive; Milwaukee historians Gregory Filardo and Hugh Swofford; author John Gurda, for his courtesy and support; Christine Morrow, head librarian of the periodicals desk, Milwaukee Public Library, for her staff's assistance and cooperation; Carlo Petrick of the Marcus Corporation; Virginia Schwartz and the humanities room staff at the Milwaukee Public Library; and Keith Spore, former publisher of the *Milwaukee Journal Sentinel,* for giving us unrestricted access to the newspaper's vast archives. A special note of gratitude goes to Milwaukee theater and architectural historian James Rankin, for his valuable assistance and editorial suggestions as we prepared this manuscript.

Thanks to the late Albert Kuhli for befriending us in 1984 and generously allowing the publication of his theater photographs.

A very special note of appreciation goes to former Milwaukee theater manager Karl Thiede, for rescuing hundreds of theater photos from destruction in the 1960s and for allowing some of them to be published here for the very first time.

Last but not least, we are indebted to editors Kate Thompson and Sara Phillips at the Wisconsin Historical Society Press for seeing this project through to completion. Their belief in the book and unswerving dedication to making it happen is the reason you're holding it today. We would also like to thank Rick Pifer, John Nondorf, John Zimm, and Erica Schock of the Wisconsin Historical Society for research assistance.

INTRODUCTION

Alhambra facade at night, 1910. Photo by J. Robert Taylor; WHS Image ID 38906

As Milwaukee celebrates more than 110 years of movie exhibition, we're grateful for the opportunity to issue this fully revised history of the city's movie palaces. Twenty years ago, when we wrote the predecessor to this book, *Milwaukee Movie Palaces,* it was our hope that readers would remember with pleasure the grandeur of a bygone age. Today, given the growing interest in restoring some of Milwaukee's first movie houses, we hope a new generation of readers will be introduced to—and intoxicated by—the images and history that took hold of our hearts many years ago.

With even fewer of the original theaters standing, this history is more important than ever. It's more than just the theater buildings that are disappearing. Gone is a time when people sat on their front porch on a summer evening and greeted neighbors walking home from the theater down the block. Our memories of Milwaukee movie palaces and neighborhood theaters consist of more than just starry ceilings, plush seats, and elaborate decor—they are a link to an age of romance, of innovation, and of community. We hope readers seize the chance to relive their own favorite moments spent gazing up at the silver screen. And we hope, too, that the publication of this book helps ensure that our old theaters, especially the ones that have long vanished from the landscape, will remain forever embedded in our collective memory.

The history of Milwaukee cinema began long before the advent of the movie palace. The years just before motion pictures were invented were full of entertainment options for an eager public. Panoramas, dime museums, operas and musical shows in summer beer gardens, and blood-and-thunder stage melodramas were just some of what kept Victorian-era minds amused. Fast-forward ten years, to the infancy of what we now refer to as nickel theaters, or nickelodeons, often nothing more than a storefront outfitted with a white sheet for a screen and some benches for seating. No wonder Milwaukee's upper crust refused to set foot in these places. But even they couldn't stay away for long. Motion pictures suddenly seemed to appeal to everyone, and almost overnight newer, cleaner, better theaters sprang up at commercial intersections all over the city. Admission was now an expensive ten cents, but that didn't stop people from coming. Audiences rushed enthusiastically to see love stories, thrillers, comedies, and Westerns. They began to recognize certain players, too, such as Mary Pickford, the Gish sisters, and Charlie Chaplin.

Fast-forward again. By 1926 the movies began to talk. When audiences got a taste of seeing their favorite stars performing along with synchronized sound, the days of silent pictures accompanied by organ or piano were over. Going to the movies became a total audio and visual sensory experience, and the theaters built during this time reflected that. The new theaters were considered "palaces" because, in addition to several thousand seats, they incorporated exotic Arabian, Indian, and Oriental themes that added to moviegoers' sense of escape. For this is really what going to the movies was all about, especially for a nation in the grip of the Great Depression. Troubles would still be there when patrons came out of the theater, but for a few hours they could live in a world where people didn't worry about how they were going to feed their families or pay the light bill.

By 1900, dime museums had all but disappeared from the landscape. In Milwaukee, the years 1883 to 1897 marked the heyday of this nineteenth-century entertainment phenomenon.
Milwaukee Sentinel

The movie palaces entertained audiences until the post–World War II economy made it possible for young families to own their own homes in newly created suburbs of the city. Before long, the movie theaters followed them, leaving the once-grand palaces to fall into disrepair.

What you're about to read is the history of Milwaukee's theaters, from the 1890s to the grand theaters of the Roaring Twenties to the shopping mall cracker boxes of

Third Street Looking South from Wells Street,

Milwaukee, Wis.

In 1911, the Princess and the American Theaters stood side by side on North Third Street between Wisconsin and Wells. Larry Widen Collection

today. It's a tale that isn't over yet; in the past two decades, the revival of interest in preservation and restoration of theaters has confirmed that there's still life in these grand old palaces. As you turn these pages and examine the captivating images spanning more than a century, we hope you will come to appreciate the legacy of the movie theater.

Larry Widen Collection

SILVER SCREENS

ONE

BEFORE THE MOVIES: 1842–1900

"You must have been warned against letting the golden hours slip by; but some of them are golden only because we let them slip by."—J. M. Barrie, creator of Peter Pan

From 1852, when Milwaukee's first gas streetlight was installed, until 1880, when electric lights were placed in the Newhall House Hotel, city streets, public buildings, and private residences were lit by natural gas. Although a mere mention of the word *gaslight* evokes a romanticized image of a time when life was slower and people lounged in parlors or sitting rooms illuminated by golden light, the reality of daily life for Milwaukee residents during the gaslight era was often more difficult than nostalgic reminiscing would suggest.

Packs of wild dogs ran rampant through the streets of downtown, foraging for food. Pedestrians, particularly ladies whose skirts brushed the ground, routinely dodged heaps of horse manure. Large mud holes on major thoroughfares were often filled with sewer water and dead fish, causing unsavory, if not unsanitary, conditions.

With challenges such as these, it's no wonder the citizens of early Milwaukee looked for a few hours of entertainment when the opportunity arose. In 1842, the city's population numbered only 2,100; still, an enterprising showman named John Hustis sensed a need for a theater in which popular dramas of the day could be performed. Hustis's theater, located at North Third Street and Juneau Avenue, was a rustic frame building with hard wooden benches and tallow candle illumination. On a September evening, a handful of patrons braved a treacherous, vile-smelling quagmire on Third Street to attend a performance of *The Merchant of Venice* given by an acting troupe from Chicago. The theater offered two seasons of drama before it

Stagehands at an unidentified Milwaukee theater, 1905. Photo by Harry Lyman

burned to the ground, the fire generating from one of the many lanterns used to illuminate the stage. Having lost his desire to continue in the theater business, John Hustis retired to build a home in Hustisford, Wisconsin, the town he founded.

With the Hustis theater defunct, plays were offered at the Milwaukee Saloon, a hall on Broadway near East Wisconsin Avenue. In 1846, Chicago theater man John B. Rice presented dramas at Military Hall on East Wells Street. Although Military Hall was less than adequate as a performing stage, it sufficed for two years until Rice was able to open a new theater on Broadway. (When Rice's Broadway Street theater burned in 1850, he returned to Chicago, where he was later elected mayor.) Also in operation at this time were Gardener's Hall at Water and Wisconsin, John Ryan's Gaiety Theater on Broadway, and Albany Hall on East Michigan Street, all of which offered varying forms of musical and dramatic entertainment.

Most of these theaters burned down in the early 1850s, coinciding with the introduction of gaslight illumination for public streets and buildings. Although the new, natural gas illumination was superior to candles and lanterns, gas lighting was not without problems. Explosions and other fiery mishaps were commonplace in these theaters. One of them, Young's Hall, actually burned down twice. Proprietor William Young eventually constructed his third theater out of brick in 1860 at the corner of Milwaukee and Michigan Streets. In 1865, the 1,400-seat hall was renamed the Academy of Music, and it would survive for another sixty years.

A permanent theater company had yet to establish itself in town, and so amuse-

E. Karl's Vaudeville Family Theater Co.

NORTH SIDE TURN HALL—1025 WALNUT ST.

SUNDAY, OCT. 1 MATINEE 2:30 EVENINGS 8 P. M.

Entire New Programme for To-day

MIKADO—Madrigal and Fan Dance. VIENNA GIRLS—Original Austrian Duet. KATE KARL, MARIE ROSA, FRANCES LEVY—The Baby Wonder. Dramatic Songs and Coon Impersonators and JESSIE, The Baby Wonder's 6-year-old Sister, Salvation Army, Comical Duet, ADOLPH KAPPEL, the Famous Comedian. THE GAMBLER'S FATE—A Dramatic Scene of the Early Days in the Far West.

Admission 10 and 25c. Reserved Seats 10c Extra

The North Side Turn Hall, at Tenth and Walnut, was a vaudeville theater before Henry Trinz and his brothers bought it and renovated the building into a motion picture theater called the Columbia. This ad highlights several acts typical for the vaudeville stage.
Milwaukee Sentinel

ment hall owners relied on traveling companies to perform on their stages. In those days, itinerant actors considered themselves lucky to have their room and board covered. More often than not, the meager box office receipts meant the actors were stranded in town until the theater owner collected enough money to send them on their way. Bully Foster, a popular actor of the time, actually pawned his pocket watch to settle his debts before he was able to leave town.

In Milwaukee's theater infancy, the performances were always in English. However, by 1852, the city's population was more than twenty thousand people, nearly half of whom were of German descent. Almost overnight there was a market for a theater that offered productions in the alternative language. Musician Joseph Kurz and his family first presented German musical comedies in Mozart Hall, located at Eighth and Wells Streets. The following year, Kurz opened his own theater on the top floor of the old City Hall Building, the site of the present City Hall. The Kurz family wrote music, painted scenery, built sets, and even acted as their own press agents. Because they were the first to use a newspaper ad to promote their shows, Milwaukee's first theater advertising was in German.

Tickets to the Kurz shows, such as *Two Gentlemen and One Servant* and *The Dead Nephew,* were fifty cents for the main floor and twenty-five cents in the mezzanine. Money was not accepted at the theater, and tickets for shows were available in advance only at authorized locations such as Leuddemann's Restaurant or Ott's Bookstore. With the financial backing of prominent businessmen, Joseph Kurz emerged as the founding father of Milwaukee's German theater movement, which would flourish until it was quashed by the anti-German sentiment of World War I. The Kurz family's crowning achievement was the construction of the thousand-seat Stadt Theater in 1868, an opulent stage located at Third and Kilbourn that was devoted exclusively to the German theater.

By 1872, English-speaking patrons flocked to performances by high-quality traveling theater companies at Jacob Nunnemacher's elegant Grand Opera House, situated on the present site of the Pabst Theater.

Because Shakespeare, opera, and other classical theater performances did not appeal to everyone in Milwaukee, a variety of other entertainment forms sprang up to accommodate all levels of taste and income. Thus, residents were able to spend their spare time at the inexpensive amusement parks, dime museums, and panorama halls.

Panoramas were a short-lived but extremely popular entertainment phenomenon that began in the 1880s. Oil paintings, often hundreds of feet long, were shown to an audience as a narrator explained each scene. These paintings took several hours

The Pabst: The Best of the German-American Theater Tradition

Pabst's Stadt Theater, 1891. WHS Image ID 37232

The Pabst Theater has reigned over the corner of Wells and Water Streets since 1895. The Pabst is actually the second theater to occupy the site; the Swiss-immigrant Nunnemacher brothers opened their Grand Opera House there in 1871. Frederick Pabst, a former Great Lakes steamship captain and head of the Pabst Brewing Company, purchased the theater from the Nunnemachers in 1890, named it Das Neue Deutsche Stadt-Theater ("The New German City Theater"), and had it remodeled and decorated in a more Germanic style.

The Stadt Theater was destroyed by fire in January 1895 while Pabst was vacationing in Europe. When informed of the disaster, Pabst cabled back with the now-famous reply: "Rebuild at once!" Pabst's favorite

architect, Otto Strack, constructed the innovative replacement theater to be virtually fireproof. "The current Pabst theater was built in the footprint of the old opera house," according to local movie theater historian Jim Rankin. "But it's made completely of iron, steel, tile and concrete, so there's nothing that will burn."

The new theater, now called the Pabst, opened on November 9, 1895. A troupe of actors traveled from Berlin to perform *Zwei Watten*, or "Two Coats of Arms," said to be a German version of *An American Cousin*, the play Abraham Lincoln had been enjoying at Ford's Theatre when he was assassinated thirty years earlier. The Pabst hosted many German touring companies until World War I, after which nearly all of

The Pabst: The Best of the German-American Theater Tradition

its productions were in English. With the advent of motion pictures, the Pabst became a "mixed-use" venue, featuring both films and live performaces.

A number of international stars have graced the theater's stage over the past century, including Enrico Caruso, Marlene Dietrich, John Philip Sousa, George M. Cohan, Helen Hayes, Sir Laurence Olivier, Sarah Bernhardt, and Katharine Hepburn. Wisconsin actors Alfred Lunt and Lynn Fontanne "considered the Pabst their 'home' theater," said Rankin. "They made a point to begin and end every season with a performance there."

The Pabst Brewery owned the theater until 1953, at which time a foundation representing Lynde Bradley, Allis-Chalmers, and Froedtert monies assumed con-

trol. In 1961 the foundation sold the theater to the city of Milwaukee. The city completed a major overhaul in 1976 that restored much of its original style. In 1989 the city annexed the Pabst Theater to the Wyndham Hotel and the Milwaukee Center office tower, making it an integral part of the Milwaukee Center complex. In the mid-1990s the theater's board of directors renamed it the Captain Frederick Pabst Theater. The city sold the Pabst to local entrepreneur Michael Cudahy in 2002, with the stipulation that Cudahy would invest funds to make the showplace a competitive venue. Even more satisfying is the way the theater's legacy intertwines the Pabsts and the Cudahys, two of Milwaukee's founding families, more than a century later.

to unroll as they moved from one large wooden spool to another accompanied by live music. Panoramas were the forerunners of moving pictures because of the subjects of the paintings—famous battles, fires, and religious scenes, such as *The Expulsion of Adam and Eve from Paradise*—as well as the manner in which they were exhibited. The first panorama paintings were shown in music halls and theaters by traveling companies that specialized in their presentation.

The panoramas soon became popular enough to warrant a permanent showplace, and the Panorama was built at North Sixth Street and Kilbourn Avenue. A group of German painters settled in Milwaukee in 1885 to paint panoramas that would be shown in this building and would then tour the United States. These massive canvases often took a dozen artists six to eight months to complete at a total cost of more than twenty-five thousand dollars.

For the more famous paintings, such as *General Grant's Assault on Vicksburg,* extensive research was done, and several artists were sent to the battle site to sketch the actual terrain. After the drawings were completed, they were projected onto a canvas, and the images were drawn and painted. The final step before opening to the public was to add rocks, trees, fences, and actual soil in front of the painting to create a realistic, three-dimensional diorama. The result was a painted canvas 50 feet high and 350 to 400 feet long that would be on continual exhibit for a year or more in the panorama building.

Left: This image of Plankinton Avenue looking north from Wisconsin was taken in the late 1880s. The People's Theater was one of a few establishments that provided an economically priced alternative to seeing a show at one of the city's legitimate stages. Photo by Julian Stein

Above: Panorama paintings were exhibited in circular buildings due to the way the paintings were unveiled to audiences. *Milwaukee Sentinel*

Below left: Panorama artist and model. Milwaukee County Historical Society

On July 4, 1885, the depiction of *Grant's Assault* was unveiled to an enthusiastic public, who gladly paid fifty cents each to view it. Coincidentally, the newspapers were running headlines that Grant was dying in New York at the same time the panorama was opening in Milwaukee. Inside the panorama, lecturer James Larkin gave a thrilling account of the Vicksburg battle. As he told the story, the appropriate section of the huge canvas was illuminated, drawing the audience's attention to that particular scene. The talk continued in this manner until all areas of the canvas had been exposed.

Despite the panoramas' initial popularity, the novelty was worn out by 1890. And when motion pictures were projected in 1896, any hopes of a panorama revival were dashed. Several Milwaukee artists went to California in 1899 to produce a version of *Dewey's Victory at Manila Bay*, but its appeal was fleeting. The painters sustained themselves by creating murals for the Milwaukee Turner Hall

Above: Frank Trottman managed the Star Dime Museum and several other theaters in the late nineteenth century. After 1900, his show business background helped him to become one of Milwaukee's pioneer motion picture men. By 1905, Trottman was operating the Gem on South Fifth Street. Milwaukee Public Library

Right: The Star, located on Plankinton and Michigan, was originally a dime museum. The building was torn down in 1910 to make way for the expansion of Gimbel Brothers Department Store. Larry Widen Collection

walls; building stage scenery for the Pabst, Alhambra, and Bijou Theaters; and accepting private commissions. Today, one Milwaukee panorama survives; *The Battle of Atlanta* is on permanent display in a museum in Atlanta's Grant Park, presented in much the same way as it was in 1895.

The dime museum, another popular but short-lived form of amusement, was a hybrid of museum, circus sideshow, and theater. The concept of the dime museum originated with P. T. Barnum's American Museum, opened in 1841 in lower Manhattan. By the 1880s there was a similar venue in every large city east of the Mississippi. Named for the ten-cent standard admission price, dime museums offered

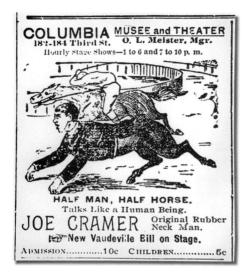

COLUMBIA MUSEE and THEATER
182-184 Third St.   O. L. Meister, Mgr.
Hourly Stage Shows—1 to 6 and 7 to 10 p. m.

HALF MAN, HALF HORSE.
Talks Like a Human Being.
JOE CRAMER   Original Rubber
Neck Man.
New Vaudeville Bill on Stage.
ADMISSION............10c   CHILDREN..............5c

Above: Before the advent of motion picture theaters, Milwaukeeans often whiled away an afternoon or evening in one of the city's dime museums. Named for their standard price of admission, this unique combination of freak show, vaudeville stage, and traditional museum featured countless attractions on weekly handbills that spared no hyperbole.
Milwaukee Sentinel

Right: Otto Meister was a shipping clerk with a promising future in 1892 when he went to work at the Wonderland Dime Museum on Third Street.
Frances Maertz Collection

exhibits that might be found in a traditional public museum. However, the real allure was the morbid fascination found in the ever-changing "sideshow" program of midgets, giants, people without arms or legs, extremely heavy or thin men and women, and other unusual individuals that performed in one way or another. An armless woman painted pictures with a brush held between her toes; a man who was tattooed on every inch of his skin disrobed to show highly detailed and accurate historical images. These shows and performers changed on a weekly basis.

In March 1884, a young theatrical entrepreneur named Jacob Litt was appointed manager of the Schlitz Park Theater. The park, located at Seventh and Walnut Streets, was a favorite summer place to hear music and opera. In addition to booking a season of concerts for the Park Theater, Litt established a small museum adjoining the park's opera house.

Litt used his profit from the Schlitz Park museum to purchase the failing Grand Avenue Dime Museum at Second Street and Wisconsin Avenue, across from the Plankinton House Hotel. He completely overhauled and repainted the interior, adding private boxes on either side of the stage. Litt ran the museum successfully for the next five years, with attractions that included "The Turtle Boy—Queerest, Quaintest Atom of Humanity Ever on Display," "The Bewitching Albino Sisters Whose Flowing White Hair Reaches Below Their Waists," "The Dog-Faced Boy," and "Belle Moody, the Human Billiard Ball." Litt also presented "The Bloodless Vivisectionist," an elegantly garbed magician named Dr. Lynn, who performed in 1885. Onstage, Lynn produced a series of long, gleaming knives and appeared to dismember a living human being before the audience's eyes. With a flourish, the man then replaced his victim's limbs and head, apparently none the worse for wear. Eleven-year-old Ehrich Weiss, the future Harry Houdini, was sitting in the audience. Mesmerized by Lynn's act, he later said it was this performance that inspired him to become an illusionist.

Several years later, in 1892, a frustrated young actor/comedian named Otto Meister, born in Milwaukee in 1869, left his job as clerk for the Goodrich Transportation Company and found work in taverns and music halls as a German-dialect comedian and as a barker at the newly opened Wonderland Museum on North Third Street. Soon Meister was working inside as an assistant manager as well as a featured performer. His specialty was stand-up comedy done with an exaggerated

(continued on page 14)

Jacob Litt: Milwaukee's Forgotten Showman

"Running a museum is the hardest work I've ever done. If anyone says otherwise, I'll hit him, pay the fine, and exhibit him as The World's Biggest Liar."
—Jacob Litt, 1884

Jacob Litt, Milwaukee's leading theatrical magnate of the late nineteenth century, is all but forgotten today. The stocky, mustachioed showman worked his way up from exhibiting frauds and hoaxes in a dime museum to owning a chain of legitimate theaters that flourished in five major cities. A millionaire by the age of thirty-five, he was dead of overwork just ten years later. Litt was a pioneer showman whose theater management practices were copied by legendary East Coast owners like B. F. Keith.

Future showman Jacob Isaac Lit, the son of Dutch Jews who came to the United States in 1855, was born on March 19, 1860. Like a number of his classmates, Litt left school around age twelve to get a job. Too frail to work in one of the city's steamy factories, he became a program boy at the newly opened Grand Opera House. By age fifteen he was the venue's assistant treasurer; by twenty he was the business manager. Located on the site of the current Pabst Theater, the Grand Opera House opened on August 17, 1871. The monumental three-story theater/office/storefront complex was owned by Jacob Nunnemacher, a distiller of spirits who had become rich after the Civil War. His sons, Herman and Jacob Jr., were given management of the theater. In summer 1881, the Nunnemachers went to New York City to scout new acts, leaving Jacob Litt not only to run the theater, but to book the coming season's attractions as well.

The legitimate theaters were closed from September to May, so after a year of successfully managing the Grand Opera House, Litt tried producing outdoor summer shows at the Carney Opera House in Waukesha. To boost attendance, he chartered trains from

(continued on next page)

Top: Jacob Litt ran the Milwaukee Dime Museum on Wisconsin Avenue from 1884 to 1889. He later opened the Bijou and became a prominent producer of stage shows across the Midwest. Milwaukee County Historical Society

Above: The Grand Opera House was Milwaukee's premier stage in the 1870s and 1880s. When it burned down in 1895, owner Frederick Pabst immediately replaced the theater with the Pabst Theater on the same site. Milwaukee Public Library

Jacob Litt: Milwaukee's Forgotten Showman

SCHLITZ'S PARK.

O. OSTHOFF, LESSEE.

In the 1880s, the city's various outdoor amusement parks provided summer entertainment at an affordable price. Larry Widen Collection

(continued from page 9)

Milwaukee and other areas, a venture that earned him enough capital to help his father's ailing secondhand clothing business.

About this time, Litt received word that the Nunnemacher brothers were staying in New York indefinitely, leaving him in charge of the Grand for another year. Despite the unexpected workload, he followed through with plans for another season of his own summer shows, this time at the prestigious Schlitz Park. Owned by the Schlitz Brewing Company, the park was a popular summer beer garden and recreational haunt for city residents. Manager Otto Osthoff handled park operations and concessions and installed an ice-skating rink to generate wintertime revenue.

Litt and Osthoff formed the Bijou Theater Company in 1883 with a full summer season of light opera. In addition, Litt opened a dime museum adjacent to the park's theater. Advertised as a safe environment for

children and an educational experience for adults, the museum featured a zoo and hourly stage shows similar to circus sideshows. The Osthoff/Litt ventures at Schlitz Park were successful, and Schlitz repeated them the following year.

Litt used his share of the profits to purchase the Milwaukee Dime Museum on Wisconsin Avenue, which he renovated and reopened in September 1884. The museum was staffed with a regular lecturer, William Gore, as well as a musical director, a portrait painter, a scenic artist, an animal master, two property men, a doorkeeper, an advertising agent, and two managers. Police officers were placed on retainer to patrol the museum during operating hours, preserve order, and eject men who repeatedly annoyed female patrons. During the 1884–1885 season, the Milwaukee Dime Museum netted seventeen thousand dollars. Litt estimated eighty-three thousand people visited the museum during the first month of operation.

In September 1885, Schlitz Brewing officials discontinued the summer music series in Schlitz Park, feeling certain they could earn more revenue by using the park for parties and picnics. Osthoff went on to become a promoter of panorama paintings and opened the Osthoff Hotel in Elkhart Lake, a venture he ran until his death in 1917.

Without a venue for his musicals, Litt acquired the lease for the financially ailing Academy of Music. With the support of the Milwaukee Musical Society, an organization that sponsored concerts and opera presentations, Litt invested ten thousand dollars to breathe new life into a theater that had financially

Jacob Litt: Milwaukee's Forgotten Showman

broken every manager ever associated with it. When the newly renovated Academy opened in the fall of 1885, the seats were competitively priced and shows were targeted to a new audience—one that enjoyed melodramas with sneering villains, clean-cut heroes, deadly sawmill blades, and heroines tied to railroad tracks, much to the Musical Society's chagrin. These popular attractions, however, kept audiences on the edge of their seats and Litt's books in the black.

Although Litt's museum and tenure at the Academy of Music were successes, he longed to have a legitimate theater of his own. His first step toward that goal was disassociation from the tawdry world of the dime museums. A Milwaukee capitalist, John Johnston, helped make Litt's dream a reality by agreeing to a ten-year lease on a Second Street property that was to be made over into a middle-class, neighborhood-friendly theater. In March, Litt began construction on the Bijou. The plans called for red pressed Anderson brick to create the Romanesque exterior facade. An elegant porte cochere at the entrance acted as a visual transition from the Romanesque exterior to the theater's Moorish-inspired interior. The proscenium arch, flanked by heavily clustered columns, called attention to the curtain, upon which was a reproduction of the Jean-Louis Gerome 1870 painting *The Sword Dance*. The curtain alone cost Litt one thousand dollars. The azure auditorium ceiling was inlaid with hundreds of incandescent lights to resemble stars. Amid them were classically rendered paintings of mythological figures. The seats were upholstered in dark blue brocade. For added luxury, each seat had a small, coin-operated peanut machine affixed to the back. With eight private boxes, the total seating capacity of the romantically appointed Bijou was 2,200.

The Bijou Opera House opened to Milwaukee's

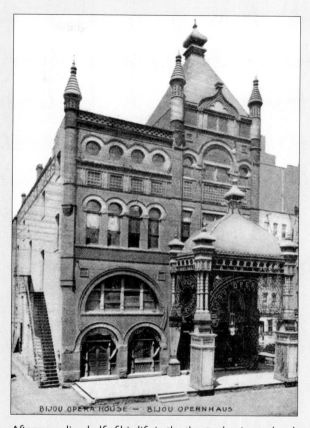

BIJOU OPERA HOUSE — BIJOU OPERNHAUS

After spending half of his life in the theater business, local impresario Jacob Litt opened his Bijou Opera House in 1889 when he was only twenty-nine years old. Larry Widen Collection

theatergoers on Saturday evening, August 17, 1889. Present at the opening was Mayor Thomas H. Brown, who insisted on pronouncing the theater's name as "By Joe."

Referred to as "the citadel of melodrama" and "the newsboy's delight," Jacob Litt's Bijou was the opera house where no opera ever played—a direct predecessor to the movie palaces of the 1920s. The mainstay

(continued on next page)

Jacob Litt: Milwaukee's Forgotten Showman

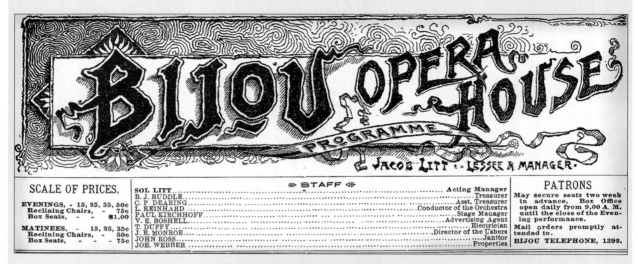

Bijou program, 1890. Larry Widen Collection

(continued from page 11)
was blood-and-thunder cliffhanger melodrama, and Litt served it up with gusto. Seats in the gallery were fifteen cents, the balcony twenty-five cents, and the main floor fifty cents. A reclining chair down in front sold for seventy-five cents, and box seats were one dollar.

Interestingly, the Bijou was the site of an early racial controversy almost as soon as it went up. In 1889, the theater refused to seat a black customer with white customers and in a separate incident would not admit a black patron through its doors. The case was brought before the state legislature in 1890 by Milwaukee's first black lawyer, William T. Green, and tried by Circuit Judge D. H. Johnson. Johnson ruled in favor of the plaintiffs: Jacob Litt was liable for damages, and African Americans were entitled to enter all public entertainment venues from that point forward. Five years later, the legislature extended black civil rights to restaurants, bars, hotels, and public transportation.

(Even though these laws were on the books, it didn't mean they were enacted. In Milwaukee, segregation was never legal but it was common practice.)

The controversy didn't stop Litt's new theater from thriving. Averaging a profit of five thousand dollars per week at the Bijou, Litt was able to establish other theaters across the Midwest. In 1890, he opened the Bijou and Lyceum Theaters in Minneapolis and the Grand Opera House and Metropolitan Theater in St. Paul. He also took a ten-year lease on the Standard Theater in Chicago. He presented some of the era's biggest moneymakers, including the Swedish dialect comedy *Yon Yonson* and *In Old Kentucky*, the perennial state fair week favorite.

While staging a production of *Shenandoah* in 1895, Litt met and married Ruth Carpenter, one of the play's stars. In 1897, he opened the McVickers Theater in Chicago with a revival of *Shenandoah*, followed by *Ben-Hur* and *Quo Vadis*. Litt installed his twenty-six-year-old nephew, Solomon, the son of his sister Mary and

Jacob Litt: Milwaukee's Forgotten Showman

deceased cousin Isaac, as manager of the Chicago venue. He then assumed control of the Broadway Theater in New York City, placing Alexander Dingwall, whom he had taken in as a full partner, in charge. He added theaters in Buffalo, Cleveland, and Philadelphia to the circuit shortly after. In 1897, Litt and his wife left Milwaukee and moved to a mansion in Manhattan. A son, Jacob Jr. (Jack), was born in 1898, and a second son, Willard David, followed two years later.

After the turn of the century, demand for the melodramas lessened, and Litt and Dingwall began offering vaudeville and burlesque at their theaters. They even became early exhibitors of motion pictures. At the end of a seven-unit vaudeville show at the Milwaukee Bijou, Litt showed the short films *Pictures of the*

Williamsburg Bridge and *Hudson by Night* as the audience left for the evening.

In 1902, Litt's physicians diagnosed severe hypertension and recommended he withdraw from the day-to-day stress of business. Litt could not bring himself to slow down, and on September 27, 1905, he suffered a stroke and died in a Yonkers, New York, sanitarium. He was forty-six years old. Leon Wachsner, the Pabst Theater manager and Litt's brother-in-law, received news of his death by telegraph. Milwaukee's former dime museum magnate and melodrama king left behind his theaters, an estate that totaled $1.25 million, and a corporation headed by Dingwall and Solomon Litt that continued to produce shows in the name of Jacob Litt for the next ten years.

Because the Bijou staged popular cliff-hangers and melodramas, it was one of the few stages in Milwaukee that did not have to convert to motion pictures. Photo by J. Robert Taylor; WHS Image ID 38905

German accent and a large walking stick. Several weeks into the 1893 season, Meister hired an act called "The Houdini Brothers and the Mystery Box" for a weeklong stand at the museum. Ehrich Weiss, now seventeen, and his younger brother Theo performed an illusion in which they switched places inside a locked box right in front of the audience. Meister and Weiss became lifelong friends as a result of their meeting that year.

Houdini: Manacled in Milwaukee

ON A BRIGHT OCTOBER MORNING IN 1897, a young man walked into Milwaukee's police headquarters and asked to see the handcuffs used to shackle prisoners. After a brief examination, he exclaimed the cuffs were worthless. With prodding from the crime reporters who frequented the halls of the station, the captain on duty was persuaded to handcuff the man. "Just one set?" the young man chuckled. "Better lock me up with everything you have." Shaking his head, the captain obliged. Smiling, the man turned his back to the growing crowd. Forty seconds later, he raised his arms in triumph as numerous sets of regulation police handcuffs clattered to the floor. While the onlookers gasped in amazement, the young man introduced himself. "My name is Harry Houdini. Don't miss my magic show tonight at the dime museum." The stunt produced the desired effect; evening editions of the papers mentioned his ability to bewilder the police, while subsequent issues ran favorable reviews of his show.

By the time of his Milwaukee appearance in 1897, the twenty-three-year-old Houdini was already a seasoned veteran of circuses, dime museums, beer halls, and even Chicago's Columbian Exposition. His extraordinary career would extend from the lowest form of theatrical venue, the dime museum, to the pinnacle of show business, headlining the famed Orpheum vaudeville circuit. Milwaukee was not a new venue to the rising star; it was in Milwaukee that he was introduced to the business, first as an audience member and later as a young performer.

Born Ehrich Weiss in 1874 in Budapest, Hungary, the future Houdini immigrated to the United States with his family before he was a year old, living first in Appleton, Wisconsin. In 1883 the family moved to Milwaukee in hopes of securing a job for Ehrich's father, a rabbi. Work prospects were dim, however, and Ehrich and his younger brother Theo took to Milwaukee's streets as bootblacks and newspaper sellers to help support the household. Years later, Houdini wrote about his boyhood in Milwaukee: "Such hardship and hunger became our lot that the less said on the subject, the better." Despite this grim sentiment, it was in Milwaukee that Houdini gave his first public performance. On October 28, 1883, he asked to perform in Jack Hoefler's Five-Cent Circus. Seeing the value of a local boy on the bill, the circus advertised the nine-year-old as "Erich, The Prince of the Air." He appeared as a contortionist and trapeze performer several more times with Hoefler's circus, later shortening his name to Eric the Great.

Houdini left Milwaukee in 1886 but returned sporadically between 1892 and 1898 to perform at Milwaukee's numerous dime museums with Theo in an act they called "The Houdini Brothers and the Mystery Box." In 1894, Theo was replaced by an even more able assistant, Harry's wife, Bess Rahner, whose slim frame allowed her to perform the Mystery Box illusion, now labeled "Metamorphosis," with ease. "The Houdinis" traveled the country until 1900, first as a sideshow attraction with the Welsh Brothers Circus and then

Throughout the 1890s, Otto Meister exhibited the "Skating Horse," the "Armless Landscape Painter," the "Legless Acrobat," and the "Iron-Skulled Man," who broke bricks on his head. In addition to the oddities and curiosities, there were endless numbers of mind readers, magicians, balladeers, speedy whittlers and clay modelers, dancers, gymnasts, musicians, and elocutionists. Soon, however, the dime museums had run their course, and their popularity began to wane. Considered by

Houdini: Manacled in Milwaukee

ONE WEEK COM. NEXT **MONDAY MATINEE**

MILWAUKEE'S OWN

HOUDINI

The Justly World Famous Self Liberator

Presenting the Most Remarkable Performance of his Strenuous Career

HARRY HOUDINI

Harry Houdini was an international star when he returned to Milwaukee to play the Majestic in 1912. Milwaukee Public Library

with the American Gaiety Girls burlesque troupe. They traveled Wisconsin extensively as a featured act at the Belle City Opera House in Racine, the Crescent Opera House in Kenosha, Germania Hall in Menasha, the Opera House in Appleton, the Myers in Janesville, and the Opera House in Beloit.

In 1900, the couple sailed to London with the promise of a booking made through London's Alhambra Theatre, an escape challenge at Scotland Yard. The one-week booking soon turned to twelve and was followed by similar successes across Europe and even in

Moscow. By 1904, Houdini was the highest-paid performer in Europe. He was much in demand when he returned to the United States in 1905. But Houdini did not perform in Milwaukee again until April 1912, when he started a weeklong stand headlining seven acts of vaudeville at the Majestic Theatre. Twice daily he performed a routine consisting of magic tricks and handcuff escapes. During his week in Milwaukee, Houdini granted numerous interviews with newspaper writers and conducted tours of his boyhood haunts. He told reporters about stealing eggs with Theo and cooking them over a makeshift fire on the roof of the Plankinton House. He also recalled selling issues of the *Milwaukee Sentinel* featuring stories of the disastrous Newhall House fire in 1883. He even posed for pictures by the Milwaukee River, where he first taught himself to stay underwater for minutes at a time.

Houdini's success at the Majestic was topped by a stunt that very nearly turned out to be his last: the death-defying escape from a padlocked steel milk can filled to the brim with water. To make the act more interesting, Houdini had accepted a challenge from the employees of Milwaukee's Schlitz Brewing Company to replace the water with beer. Fully submerged in the liquid and padlocked inside the container, the magician was nearly overcome by alcohol fumes as he worked to free himself. The audience waited with bated breath as two, then two and a half minutes passed, an assistant standing by with a fire ax in hand, ready to

(continued on next page)

Houdini: Manacled in Milwaukee

(continued from page 15)

smash the padlocks. Then, at precisely the three-minute mark—a full minute past his standard escape time—a dripping-wet Houdini emerged unsteadily from the can while the crowd shouted its approval. The great escape artist had done it again.

In addition to his stage act, magician Harry Houdini also made a number of action pictures such as *The Grim Game*, which played at the Princess in 1916.
Milwaukee Sentinel

Houdini returned to Milwaukee for an engagement at the Palace Orpheum Theater in late September 1923. At the age of forty-nine, his once-elastic physique was beginning to show signs of the incredible abuse he had heaped on it. Nevertheless, he performed the dime museum trick "Metamorphosis" with surprising agility and speed. He also mystified his audiences with the "Hindu Needle Trick," an illusion in which he placed fifty large sewing needles in his mouth, pulling them out moments later on a ten-yard strand of thread. But the highlight of his week was the Friday evening show, in which he accepted a prearranged challenge from Sheriff Phil C. Westfahl.

In a similar scenario to the one played out twenty-six years earlier at the Milwaukee police headquarters, Houdini brought the sheriff and deputies onto the stage, where they proceeded to strap the master magician in a straitjacket from head to toe. The lawmen stepped aside, the band began to play, and Houdini went to work. Within seconds, he had slipped out of the first set of ropes. He kept his back to the audience, and they were unable to see the grimace of pain crossing his features as he dislocated first one and then the other shoulder. A minute later the job was complete. "Sheriff Westfahl," Houdini said with a smile, "these are the ties that *don't* bind." Accepting a graceful defeat, the sheriff shook Houdini's hand as the crowd offered a standing ovation. It was the last time the magician would perform in Milwaukee.

Harry Houdini died on October 31, 1926. "When I pass on, I would rather have one line in the press than a one hundred-dollar wreath," he once said. Decades after his death, Houdini is still a household name that evokes visions of magic, mystery, and illusion.

performers to be the bottom rung of the show business ladder, the museums were viewed as a curiosity by the public, who usually did not return for a second visit. Consequently, the museums changed ownership frequently and often went out of business after several years. By the turn of the century, the museums had all but vanished from the urban landscape. Still, Meister stayed in show business his entire life, going on to open the Vaudette, Magnet, Butterfly, and White House Theaters.

When the Newhall House Hotel installed electric lighting in April 1880, enthusiastic public reaction to the innovative method of illumination spelled the beginning of the end for gas. Ironically, the fabulous hotel also burned to the ground three years later in one of the greatest disasters in the city's history. The cause of the fire, which started in the basement, was never determined, although arson was suspected. World-famous midget performer Tom Thumb, a guest in the hotel, was rescued; seventy-five other people were not as fortunate.

William Young's Academy of Music was the city's first theater to install electric lighting, in 1882. That same year saw similar electrical upgrades to the post office, the Exposition Building, Chapman's Department Store, and the Phillip Best Brewery. A contemporary newspaper account stated that the lights on Schlitz Park Theater's pagoda could be seen fourteen miles away. Wisconsin Avenue was soon lined with electric streetlights that reached from the river to Eleventh Street.

In Milwaukee, motion pictures were projected on a screen for the first time in 1896. The enthusiasm displayed by the public for these films spelled the end for attractions such as dime museums and the panoramas.
Milwaukee Sentinel

Although it would be a while before electricity completely dominated the landscape, each year saw more streets, more public buildings, and more residences accept the conversion. From an entertainment standpoint, theaters built after 1890 were beacons in the Milwaukee night, brightly lit and ready to present motion pictures after the first Vitascope motion picture was shown at the Academy of Music in July 1896.

On Sunday, July 26, 1896, the Edison Vitascope made its appearance at the Academy of Music Theater at Broadway and Michigan. The event marked the first time that a motion picture had ever been projected before a Milwaukee audience. Of the premiere, a *Milwaukee Sentinel* reviewer stated, "The Academy was liter-

(continued on page 21)

Precursors to Film

In the years before technological and scientific advances allowed photographic images to be projected on a screen, visual amusement devices ranged from simple contraptions that could be used at home to complex machinery in commercial arcades or theaters.

Magic Lantern

The Magic Lantern projected still images onto a wall or screen, much like an early slide show, and it existed centuries before the motion picture was invented. A simple device, it used images drawn (later photographed) on transparent glass plates and arranged on a cylinder. A lantern that illuminated and projected the images was in the center of the cylinder. In the nineteenth century, the Magic Lantern was a popular form of amusement, with pictures accompanying a narrated story.

Phenakistiscope

In 1833, Belgian inventor Dr. Joseph Plateau fashioned the Phenakistiscope, which used two rotating disks and a mirror to give still images the appearance of movement. The perimeter of one of the disks, adorned with a series of drawings, was rotated in front of a mirror. When viewers saw the reflected images through the second, slotted disk, the pictures appeared to be moving. Plateau based his invention on the theory that the eye retains an image in the retina for a short duration after an object is viewed. Some thought that "persistence of vision" caused a series of images viewed rapidly to blend together, giving the illusion of movement to still images. Although this theory was eventually discredited, it did inspire the creation of machines such as the Phenakistiscope that would one day lead to the motion picture camera.

Zoetrope

The Zoetrope consisted of a drum with vertical slits cut in the sides. The operator placed a succession of still pictures inside the drum, which were visible through the slits. When the drum was spun, the pictures would move fast enough to make the viewer see one long sequence of movement, not the individual images. Zoetropes first came on the market in the 1830s under a variety of brand names. In the 1860s, operators projected images from a Zoetrope onto a wall for an audience using a crude illumination device placed inside the drum.

Stereoscopes and Stereopticons

Stereo, or three-dimensional, pictures are almost as old as photography itself. In England in 1838, Charles Wheatstone patented an unwieldy system of precisely canted mirrors. By placing images beneath the mirrors, the viewer got the sensation of depth from a two-dimensional picture. Within a few years, a number of smaller systems using prisms and lenses were marketed to the public, but it wasn't until Queen Victoria professed her admiration for the stereoscope at the Crystal Palace Exposition in 1851 that stereo viewing became popular.

While not inexpensive, at least one stereoscope was to be found in nearly every middle- and upper-class American home of the time, much as television is today. The most popular stereoscope subjects were travel pictures of great cathedrals, exotic cultures, ancient ruins, and modern cities. Stereo photos also documented current events, such as the building of the Panama Canal, the horrors of the Johnstown flood and the San Francisco earthquake, and the excitement of the 1892 Chicago World's Fair and the 1904 St. Louis World's Fair.

Precursors to Film

Norwegian immigrant Andreas Larsen Dahl took stereo photographs in and around Dane County, Wisconsin, throughout the 1870s and early 1880s. He often posed families in front of their houses, along with many of their possessions. For this stereoscopic image, circa 1878, the subjects displayed their own stereoscope, along with a large doll on one woman's lap. WHS Image ID 34656; WHS Image ID 26688

Zoopraxiscope

Developed by Eadweard Muybridge in the 1870s, the Zoopraxiscope was the first machine to use high-speed photography and successive photographic images to mimic movement. In 1878 and 1879, Muybridge set up a series of cameras to photograph horses as they ran on a racetrack, hoping to determine whether all four of a horse's hooves left the ground while at a gallop. The horses set off trip wires that activated strategically placed cameras with single high-speed shutters. Muybridge then collected the photographs and displayed drawings of them on the Zoopraxiscope.

Similar in operation to the Phenakistiscope, the Zoopraxiscope used two disks that rotated in opposite directions, one fitted with images around its perimeter, the other slotted to act as a shutter. Behind the disks, a lantern provided illumination to project the images onto a screen. Muybridge lectured extensively with his device and used further series of photographs to study human movement. Shortly after meeting Muybridge

(continued on next page)

Precursors to Film

(continued from page 19)
in 1888, Thomas Edison was inspired to begin development of a camera that could take successive high-speed photographs.

Kinetoscope

Patented by Thomas Edison in 1891, the Kinetoscope (sometimes spelled Kinetascope) was a motion picture projection device for use by one person at a time. Because the viewer had to squint though a lens to view the tiny, flickering image, the invention was commonly referred to as a "peep show." The entire apparatus was housed inside a large wooden cabinet, and the Kinetoscope was popular with 1890s penny arcade owners, who often installed several units in their place of business. To keep customers coming back, owners needed a steady supply of new films. To fill this void, in December 1892 the Edison Manufacturing Company built a motion picture production studio at West Orange, New Jersey. The building was nicknamed the Black Maria because of its resemblance to the police paddy wagon of the same name. Edison constructed the studio so that it could be turned to catch the light of the sun, no matter where it was in the sky.

The earliest copyrighted film that still survives is "Edison Kinetoscopic Record of a Sneeze, January 7, 1894" (also known as "Fred Ott's Sneeze"), which captures Fred Ott, an Edison employee, sneezing comically for the camera.

Vaudeville performers became some of the first actors in these early fifteen- and thirty-second films, as did Annie Oakley and other performers from Buffalo Bill's Wild West Show. Because the films were most often viewed by men, some featured scantily clad women, boxing matches, and cockfights. Edison assistant William Kennedy Laurie Dickson made more than seventy-five of these motion pictures in 1894 alone.

Edison's Kinetoscope, one of the first motion picture projectors, was patented in 1897. This photo was taken in 1931 by commercial photographer Angus McVicar.
WHS Image ID 18417

Precursors to Film

The pioneering shot of Thomas Edison employee Fred Ott, mid-sneeze. *Harper's Weekly*, March 24, 1894

Vitascope

The single-user Kinetoscopes were profitable, but it was clear that projecting motion pictures to large audiences could reap even more money. Although Thomas Edison is credited with the invention of the Vitascope, an early motion picture–projection system, he merely owned part of the patent on its technology. Several versions of what came to be called the Vitascope appeared publicly in 1895, a full year before the Edison machine made its debut in New York City. Ultimately, the Edison Manufacturing Company purchased the rights to these competing devices to manufacture one version of the machine on the condition that it be advertised as a new Edison invention named the Vitascope. The Vitascope had its first theatrical exhibition on April 23, 1896, at Koster and Bial's Music Hall in New York City; it appeared in Milwaukee just months later. The popularity of this early prototype of today's movie projector was prophetic. In just two decades the longer-running "moving picture" would take American audiences by storm.

ally crowded to the doors at both performances yesterday, hundreds being turned away from the evening performance before 8:00 p.m. Undoubtedly, the great attendance was caused by the announcement that Edison's wonderful invention, the Vitascope, would be seen in this city for the first time."

The pictures presented included a New York City elevated train platform with arriving and departing trains, the celebrated "kiss" between Mae Irwin and John Rice from the New York stage comedy *The Widow Jones*, and a boxing match between Gentleman Jim Corbett and a hapless opponent. The *Sentinel* reporter (and the audience) appeared to be most impressed by a scene in which the surf rolled along a stone pier, the waves seeming to break in the viewer's lap.

Until the perfection of the Vitascope, only one person at a time could view the tiny, flickering Kinetoscope images in darkened penny arcades. Now, larger motion picture images could be presented to a mass audience, translating into increased revenue streams for theater owners. The rapidity and enthusiasm with which people

Edison and the Advent of Film

As Steve Neale notes in *Cinema and Technology: Image, Sound, Colour*, when Thomas Edison set out in 1887 to make "a permanent record of an indefinite number of successive movements" with a single camera, he entered a field that was in the midst of rapid progress. Building on the work of cinema's many pioneers, Edison devised a motion picture camera, the Kinetograph, and a viewer, the Kinetoscope, that brought film to audiences around the world. But while the Wizard of Menlo Park contributed much to the early film industry, Edison probably misunderstood cinema's potential. The Kinetoscope was a major step in the evolution of cinema, but Edison did not market his inventions aggressively, and he lost not just his corner on the market but his control over the technologies he had helped define.

From the beginning, Edison placed little importance on his motion picture devices. The main role of his assistant, W. K. L. Dickson, was to develop oil-refining techniques, not moving picture machines. Dickson worked on photography only when time allowed, and he was not given assistants until two years into the project. What's more, according to Neale, Edison never secured patents in Europe for the Kinetoscope or Kinetograph, which allowed others to copy his machines and improve upon them. Among Edison's imitators were the Lumière brothers, Louis and Auguste, whose Cinématographe combined the camera and projector and used only sixteen frames per second compared to the Kinetoscope's forty, and Robert Paul, whose Theatrograph was one of the most successful early movie projectors.

After he began production and distribution of Kinetograph viewers and short movies, Edison remained quiet in the emerging field of cinema. One reason for this was a renewed interest in improving

Thomas Alva Edison, 1913. WHS Image ID 9585

the phonograph he had patented in 1878, notes Paul Israel in *Edison: A Life of Invention*. Another possible reason is that Edison hoped he could secure a monopoly on cinema with his patents on the Kinetoscope and Kinetograph. The Kinetograph was a financial success, and it is likely that Edison wished to reap the profits without devoting time and energy toward improving his creations, according to Neale. Ultimately, however, Edison's lack of interest led other inventors to explore an area he had neglected: projecting films for audiences. While engineers in America and Europe worked responded to the new form of motion pictures spelled the beginning of the end for entertainments such as the dime museum.

Several local entrepreneurs were quick to recognize the potential profit from exhibiting moving pictures. The Academy of Music had several repeat performances of the Vitascope before the end of 1896, and by March 1897 the management had instituted weekly showings of films under the billing "Magnascope." In November 1897, Otto Meister presented a variety of films at his Phanta-Phone and Nickelodeon Theaters, located at 212 West Wisconsin Avenue. The Phanta-Phone was a short-lived experiment by Meister attempting to combine the acts of a dime museum with penny-operated phonograph and Kinetoscope machines, as well as the projection of a variety of moving picture scenes. The Phanta-Phone had been in business for less than two months when Meister decided to revamp it into a more conventional theater. The result was the Nickelodeon Theater, which opened just after Christmas. The Phanta-Phone and the Nickelodeon were located on the site that would later house Meister's Butterfly Theater.

Edison and the Advent of Film

out methods of projecting films on screens for large audiences, Edison refused to work on this himself. Ironically, his name became linked to one successful projector he owned only a partial patent for, the Vitascope, or the Edison Vitascope.

It wasn't until the rapid growth of the film industry in the early twentieth century that Edison returned to work on various cinematic devices, improving cameras and projectors and even addressing the new problem of finding a workable way to unite sound with movies. He also established a film studio and production company

Majestic Theatre

JAMES A. HIGLER, Mgr.   MILWAUKEE, WISCONSIN

Week of April 7th, 1913

Thomas A. Edison

Presents His Latest and Greatest Invention
TALKING MOTION PICTURES

1. "The Worm Turns."
2. "THE MASTER MIND"

With Edmund Breese and Company.
By Courtesy of Werba and Luescher.

Showing the gripping scene in the third act of the wonderful play which has run an entire season and is still running to packed houses at the Harris Theatre, New York.

Synopsis: A mysterious and unknown person called The Master Mind, because of his exceptional mentality, is the absolute ruler of the underworld. For years he has relentlessly plotted "to get" the District Attorney, who has sent his brother to the electric chair. A Chicago waif whom he adopted and sent abroad to be educated, has come home the flower of young womanhood and The Master Mind, carrying out his diabolic scheme, brings about her marriage to the District Attorney. That portion of the play presented by the Kinetophone begins two months after the wedding. The scene discloses the District Attorney's home in New York, where The Master Mind concealing his true identity, has secured the position of butler. The wife, living in dread of exposure, is completely under his control. Another of his tools is a crook who has known the wife as a girl in Chicago. He is brought to New York supposedly to crack the District Attorney's safe. The Master Mind plans a meeting between the safe-blower and the wife so that they will be trapped together, thereby completely wrecking the District Attorney's home and causing a scandal that will blast his political ambitions.

In the early years of motion pictures, a division of Thomas Edison's company made movies for distribution to national theaters.
Milwaukee Public Library

whose early films—such as the famous short of 1903, *The Great Train Robbery* were among the first to employ a director and actors. Edison's influence in early cinema, while formidable, was tempered in later years by a series of lawsuits over his original patents that threatened to undo much of the work of those who had looked to Edison as the father of early cinema technology. However this complicated his relationship with the motion picture industry, Edison's pioneering efforts are still considered a major contribution to film.

Another theatrical manager to see potential in motion pictures was Oscar Miller, who booked Biograph Studios films at the Alhambra in the summer of 1898. Entitled *Views of the Spanish American War*, the pictures were changed every three or four weeks and were an early version of the newsreels that would later become a staple on theater programs. The films, however, were later exposed as fakes, having been shot at a movie studio in New Jersey.

Left: Oscar Miller managed several theaters and an amusement park before his untimely death in 1905. Milwaukee Public Library

Below: The exterior decorations on the American Theater on North Third Street were representative of the gaudy, colorful advertising designed to bring in patrons off the street. Photo by Albert Kuhli

A CONEY ISLAND RESORT AT MINERAL SPRING PARK ON MILWAUKEE RIVER

A Great Summer Amusement Enterprise Which Will Be Started in Milwaukee the Coming Summer.

At the beginning of the twentieth century, Milwaukee had a number of large amusement parks that offered warm weather enjoyment to the public. From Memorial Day through Labor Day, city residents traveled by electric trolley to the parks for an afternoon or evening of music, theater, dancing, and thrills. Their destinations included Pabst, Blatz, and Schlitz Parks; White City; Chutes Park; and the Whitefish Bay Resort. But the biggest and brightest of the local amusement parks was a veritable wonderland located on the Milwaukee River in Shorewood. *Milwaukee Sentinel*

By 1899, moving pictures were being shown throughout the city in halls, theaters, museums, churches, and outdoor amusement parks. Milwaukee had several popular parks near the turn of the century, and all of them were early exhibitors of moving pictures. Shoot-the-Chutes Park, located on the Milwaukee River at North and Cambridge Avenues, was the first such park to feature Biograph Studios pictures in 1898 in its vaudeville house located on the grounds. Larger parks, such as Oscar Miller's Coney Island in the eastern village of Shorewood, also presented motion pictures as one of many attractions.

Miller envisioned a New York–style amusement park to accommodate city

HIPPODROME, MILWAUKEE, WIS.   6669

The Hippodrome, at Sixth and Wells, showed boxing films in addition to other entertainment. The theater was soon renovated into Dreamland, a dance hall that lasted only a few years.

Exterior images: Larry Widen Collection; ad: *Milwaukee Sentinel*

ORIGINAL
GANS-NELSON
FIGHT PICTURES AT
HIPPODROME
Last 4 preformances Today
This afternoon and Eve.
2 P. M. and 8 P. M.
Prices 25 and 50 Cents
ORIGINAL

"DREAMLAND, The Beautiful," Milwaukee, Wis.

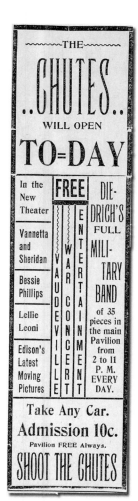

THE
..CHUTES..
WILL OPEN
TO=DAY

In the New Theater	FREE	DIE-DRICH'S
Vannetta and Sheridan	VAUDEVILLE	FULL MILI-TARY
Bessie Phillips		BAND
Lellie Leoni	WAR CONCERT	of 35 pieces in the main Pavilion from 2 to 11 P. M. EVERY DAY.
Edison's Latest Moving Pictures	ENTERTAINMENT	

Take Any Car.
Admission 10c.
Pavilion FREE Always.
SHOOT THE CHUTES

As motion pictures caught on in the final years of the nineteenth century, they often played as added attractions at amusement parks such as Chutes Park, a water attraction located on Milwaukee's lakefront.
Milwaukee Sentinel

residents. To begin construction on what was to be Milwaukee's finest outdoor amusement park, Miller found a thirty-three-acre tract of land near the 3500 block of North Oakland Avenue bounded by Menlo, Edgewood, and Oakland Avenues and the Milwaukee River to be rebuilt into his dream park.

Miller's Coney Island opened to the public on Sunday, June 10, 1900, with nearly thirty thousand in attendance. Admission to the grounds, through the Menlo Avenue gate, was free. A band concert on the lawn and a high-wire aerialist act were among the attractions that were offered at no charge. However, Coney Island's biggest rides and shows had separate ticket charges attached. The "Scenic Railway," a huge wooden roller coaster that wove through the grounds, was popular, as was the "Oriental Elephant," a massive funhouse shaped like its namesake that boasted a "haunted center," if one could find it. Beer gardens, refreshment stands, shooting galleries, games of chance, a boat launch, and a zoo rounded out the park's offerings. Coney Island also had several theaters that offered opera, vaudeville, and motion pictures.

As primitive motion pictures caught on, many traveling circuses, the state fair, and the summer parks such as White City at Fiftieth and Vliet Streets began to advertise a picture theater on the premises. Additionally, sport films such as boxing matches were now being shown in some of the city's music halls. Veteran showman John Slensby showed *Boxing Pictures Projected by the Cinematographe* in September 1899 at the Trocadero Theater on North Third Street.

Given the popularity of films, the city seemed ready for permanent structures devoted solely to motion pictures.

TWO

THE EARLIEST MOVIE THEATERS: 1901–1911

"It is a well-known fact that the nickel theater attracts a noisy and boisterous crowd, many of whom congregate on the outside of the theater before, during, and after a performance, and so demean themselves as to render residences in the same block unfit and unbearable as homes."— *Public petition to stop the opening of a theater near Mitchell Street, 1910*

As the original motion pictures slowly gained popularity in Milwaukee, a bricklayer named Max Goldstein opened a nickel theater on Wisconsin Avenue near Second Street. His theater, which opened in 1902, was the city's first permanent structure devoted exclusively to the showing of films. To promote it, Goldstein contracted with sign painters John and Thomas Saxe to prepare weekly advertising boards. Goldstein's theater did not produce enough revenue to pay all the bills, and in 1903 Saxe Signs sued him for the unpaid balance. Goldstein offered to turn the theater over to the Saxe brothers to settle the account. Initially, they planned to sell off the assets, but Thomas convinced his brother that they could make more money running the theater themselves. Under Tom Saxe's management, Goldstein's former theater ran in the black for the next two years.

In 1904, Kansas City fire chief George Hale presented an illusion that used moving pictures to create the sensation of traveling across the world. "Hale's Tours," which debuted at the St. Louis World's Fair, consisted of a platform on which were mounted fifty seats to resemble the interior of a railroad car. A device underneath gently rocked the platform to create the feeling of motion. Pictures were added, so that when the riders looked at the various scenes of the world, they felt as if they were viewing them from a train window. To add to the realism, the ticket taker acted as a

Milwaukee Journal photographer J. Robert Taylor captured this dramatic shot of the Princess at night in 1910.
Photo by J. Robert Taylor;
WHS Image ID 37666

conductor, calling out stops, ringing bells, and blowing whistles. Hale's novelty created excitement all over the country, and in Milwaukee Hale's "Tours of the World" became a popular attraction at Wonderland Amusement Park. The Saxe brothers also purchased a franchise and revamped their downtown theater to accommodate "Scenes of the World," as they called it.

John Freuler, a successful Milwaukee land broker, had his office in the prestigious Matthews Building at Third and Wisconsin. To someone of his social standing, motion pictures were considered vulgar entertainment for low-income residents who could not afford legitimate stage performances. Nevertheless, in December

Top: This rare photo shows the exterior of the Hale's Tours attraction "Tours of the World" at Wonderland Park in 1906. *Evening Wisconsin*

Above: The first Saxe theater at Second and Wisconsin underwent a number of renovations and upgrades during its nineteen-year life. Pictured here is the "Scenes of the World" from 1906.
Mary Granberg Collection

The Comique Theater, owned by John R. Freuler, was located at Kinnickinnic and Howell Avenues. Jessie Walker Collection

1905, a casual acquaintance visited John R. Freuler's real estate office, seeking a loan of four hundred dollars to open a motion picture theater. Although Freuler's friend owned a projector and a few reels of film, he wanted a permanent location from which to run shows. After listening to the pitch, Freuler agreed to the loan and made himself a half owner in the new enterprise. The two men rented a storefront at 2246 South Kinnickinnic Avenue and opened what would be Milwaukee's second permanent motion picture theater, the Comique.

By Freuler's own account, the Comique was a crude operation, with two hundred camp chairs and a piece of white muslin tacked to the wall to serve as a screen. There were no fire exits, and the ventilation was so poor that the projectionist sprayed perfume in the air at regular intervals.

For the first few weeks of operation, Freuler kept a low profile in his role as half owner, and he actually turned his head as he passed the theater, lest someone suspect his interest. Even his family was unaware of his involvement. But the Comique was a success from the beginning, and Freuler began to take an increasingly active role to the point of stopping in on a daily basis. Concerned over the constant cash short-

Stagehands from the
Crystal pose in the alley
behind the theater, 1904.
Milwaukee Public Library

age, Freuler traced the problem to the steady stream of relatives his partner was adding to the payroll. Not long after, Freuler bought the partner out and became the theater's sole owner.

A typical show at the Comique lasted about twenty minutes, and the first films presented there were rudimentary versions of comedy and chase scenes. Initially, Freuler had no control over the kinds of films he could obtain nor any guarantee as

(continued on page 36)

John Freuler and Harry Aitken: Local Boys Make Good

In 1906, a salesman called on John Freuler, owner of the Comique and Palace nickelodeons, and offered him a large variety of films that could be rented for a few days and then exchanged for new ones. This practice of exchanging films was just catching on in the industry and proved to be a great way of increasing theater attendance. The salesman who visited Freuler was Harry Aitken, an enterprising exhibitor who, along with his brother Roy, owned five nickelodeons in Chicago.

The Aitken brothers came from a farm near Goerke's Corners, east of Waukesha, Wisconsin. Enthusiastic about motion pictures, they put a makeshift theater in their barn and showed movies to patrons who sat through a presentation on their family's real estate business. Soon the Aitkens had opened several theaters in Chicago. The success of the first venture led to a string of five, all operating at a comfortable profit. They were quick to see the value in supplying films to competing theaters, a thought that had already occurred to John Freuler in Milwaukee.

Freuler and Aitken became partners and launched the Western Film Exchange, handling primarily Westerns. Soon the company had established branch offices in other markets such as Chicago, St. Louis, and Joplin, Missouri.

Over the next few years, film product became scarce as Thomas Edison filed injunctions against film studios, claiming they were in violation of his patents on cameras and projectors. In 1908, Edison made peace with nine of the pioneer film studios by forming the Motion Picture Patents Company. The monopoly allowed only MPPC-sanctioned films to be distributed and compromised the solvency of non-MPPC distributors such as Freuler and Aitken.

In 1910, Freuler and Aitken decided they would have to make their own films. They formed the American Film Manufacturing Company and began turning out quality films for distribution by Western. The MPPC employed snipers to follow the filmmakers onto location and shoot at and destroy the cameras during filming. These sneak attacks prompted Freuler to move American Film from Chicago to Santa Barbara, California. Meanwhile, Harry Aitken formed a second motion picture production company, Majestic Film. His first important acquisition for Majestic was actress Mary Pickford, who was then under contract to a rival studio. Word quickly filtered back to exchanges that many patrons were requesting more films starring "Little Mary," as her character was often called. Soon after, Aitken signed Gloria Swanson, Douglas Fairbanks, and Mabel Normand to his company's cast of players.

In March 1912, John Freuler and Harry Aitken consolidated all their operations into a corporate entity called the Mutual Film Corporation. The new company's logo featured a winged alarm clock and the legend "Mutual Movies Make Time Fly." As early as December 1913, Mutual was dominating the film industry. In Milwaukee, seventy-five theaters were showing films; of that number, twenty-seven were carrying films distributed by Mutual. After the pictures and serial episodes premiered at the Butterfly downtown, they would be routed to a network of outlying neighborhood theaters. Mutual quickly expanded beyond the Midwest, eventually providing films to more than seven thousand theaters in the United States. The company opened branch offices in London, Berlin, Rome, and Paris, all of which were overseen by Roy Aitken, Harry's brother, from the London headquarters.

(continued on next page)

John Freuler and Harry Aitken: Local Boys Make Good

(continued from page 33)

Harry Aitken's powerful negotiation skills became apparent once again when he landed a contract with filmmaker D. W. Griffith in 1913. Griffith was already considered a genius within the industry for his extraordinary understanding of light and camera movement. Still, Griffith yearned to break free of the constraints that a ten- or twenty-minute film imposed. His dream was to make a "superpicture," one that would last an hour or more. When Biograph Studios refused to authorize a longer production, Griffith went looking for a new employer. Although Paramount's Adolph Zukor offered more money, Harry Aitken lured Griffith to Mutual with the promise of artistic freedom. When the director left Biograph, he brought along actresses Dorothy and Lillian Gish.

As Mutual grew to enormous proportions, money seemed to be going out faster than ever before. At least sixty thousand dollars each week went into productions by Griffith as well as Fatty Arbuckle comedies by Mack Sennett and Westerns by Thomas Ince.

Financial concerns began when Griffith reminded Aitken of his promise to make a longer film. Griffith now envisioned this picture to run about twelve reels, or 120 minutes in length. Aitken desperately tried to convince the Mutual board of directors that backing Griffith's film *The Clansman* would be a historic milestone as well as a coup for the company.

The Mutual board included bankers and Wall Street financiers who, like Freuler, tended to be fiscally conservative. In their judgment, Griffith's proposed picture was too long, too controversial, and too expensive. Prodded by Griffith, Aitken raised nearly one hundred thousand dollars from friends and business acquaintances.

When Freuler saw a rough cut of *The Clansman*,

he knew the Mutual board had made a mistake in not backing it. When he told Aitken they would finance the entire picture, Aitken had to explain that, as president of Mutual, he had already secretly invested some of the company's money despite the board's objection. To make matters worse, Griffith had secretly sold shares in the unfinished film without Aitken's knowledge.

To bring the film back under Mutual's control, Freuler swiftly bought up twenty-five thousand dollars in notes from Griffith's and Aitken's investors who wanted a quick return on their money. Mutual board members were enraged when they learned that Griffith and Aitken had already formed the Epoch Producing Company to distribute *The Birth of a Nation*, as Griffith's film was now called. When the film premiered in Los Angeles in February 1915, it became a huge box office success, even at the astronomical price of two dollars a ticket. When the film went out on the road with traveling orchestras for extended runs in twenty major cities, the returns were staggering. The New York City engagement alone ran forty-eight weeks at the Liberty Theater on Broadway.

Furious at losing the distribution rights to *The Birth of a Nation*, the Mutual board fired Aitken. Aitken and Griffith then formed a film studio called Triangle with Mack Sennett and Thomas Ince. In Milwaukee, Aitken contracted with the Merrill Theater to play Triangle films exclusively.

As Triangle released Griffith's film *Intolerance*, the once-mighty Mutual began to have cash problems. In a desperate gamble to return the company to a position of power, in 1916 Freuler signed comedian Charlie Chaplin for an unheard-of salary of ten thousand dollars per week, plus a $150,000 signing bonus.

While Mutual hung on by its fingernails, *Intolerance*

John Freuler and Harry Aitken: Local Boys Make Good

flopped at the box office. Harry Aitken was unable to pay salaries, and stars and workers alike began departing for other studios. D. W. Griffith moved on when Triangle's Culver City studios were sold for ten cents on the dollar. The facilities, purchased by Louis B. Mayer in 1918, were the beginning of the Metro-Goldwyn-Mayer dynasty—interesting, because Mayer, a former junk dealer, had made his fortune just two years earlier as New England's regional distributor for *The Birth of a Nation*. With his limited remaining resources, Harry Aitken returned to his home in Waukesha, where he resided until his death in 1956.

As Triangle crumbled, Freuler offered Charlie Chaplin an unprecedented one million dollars to stay

An ad for *The Birth of a Nation* advertised admission prices ten times higher than those for typical movies. *Milwaukee Sentinel*

at Mutual, an offer Chaplin declined, signing instead with First National Pictures (later bought by Warner Brothers) in Burbank. Without him, Mutual's steadily declining profits led to a complete collapse of the entity in 1918. Their films and properties were absorbed by what would eventually become RKO film studios.

Despite the fantastic failure of his film enterprises, Freuler stayed in the business for several more decades, operating theaters in Milwaukee, including the White House, a theater he had opened with Otto Meister in 1916 to show Mutual films. Freuler died in 1958 at the age of eighty-six.

to when they would arrive at the theater. But crowds kept filling the Comique at a nickel a head, often to see the same films over and over again. Freuler was confident enough to invest in a second theater, the Palace, at 905 South Fifth Street.

Freuler quickly realized the real money was not in exhibition but in supplying films to other theater owners. He reasoned that if a film distributorship were located in town, exhibitors would change their programs more often. Six months later, Freuler was running the newly created Western Film Exchange out of his real estate office. Western obtained films from an exchange in Chicago and in turn rented them to storefront picture theaters as well as beer gardens, summer parks, and legitimate houses such as the Bijou, Alhambra, Crystal, and Star. Freuler encouraged local theater owners to change their film programs three, four, and even five times each week.

The first nickelodeons, named for the admission price and the Greek word for theater, *odeon,* were usually former storefronts equipped with rows of wooden benches. The more rustic operations even had dirt floors. The screen was a white wall or a sheet nailed at the corners. These picture parlors, as they were referred to on early

In late 1905, the Saxe brothers outfitted their nickel theater on Wisconsin Avenue into a motion picture attraction that simulated a trip around the world. The dazzling exterior belied the austerity inside.
Milwaukee Journal Sentinel

THE CUTEST AND NEATEST
LITTLE THEATER IN THE WORLD
OPENS THIS EVE. AT 6
VAUDETTE
THEATER
3d St., Bet. Grand Ave. and Wells St.
OPENING BILL
LITTLE TOM KUM
Japanese Contortionist.
PROF. SILVER
Up-to-Date Punch and Judy.
MISS MARIE CURTIS
Singing and Dancing Soubrette.
8--Russian Singers and Dancers--8
Also HIGH CLASS MOTION PICTURES
ADMISSION 10c.

Otto Meister opened his nickel theater, the Vaudette, on North Third Street in 1908. *Milwaukee Sentinel*

building permits, accommodated from fifty to two hundred people per show. They had little or no light, poor ventilation, and two tiny aisles in case of fire. Some of the facilities in the city's outlying areas were so primitive that during intermission the backyard or alley served as the restroom for both sexes.

Though the interiors were barren, the exteriors were garishly decorated with photos and posters and lit with hundreds of lightbulbs to attract attention. Under a Milwaukee code, theaters could not display any advertising matter in public view that contained artwork or photography of a lurid or violent nature. Women depicted in compromising situations were forbidden on any advertising material. Early theater owners who promoted their wares too enthusiastically paid fines of up to five dollars for violation of the city's billboard ordinances.

As more and more nickel theaters opened around the city, Thomas and John Saxe came to the same conclusions as John Freuler. The Hale's Tours attraction was profitable, but attendance was dwindling. Like Freuler, the brothers saw the advantage of controlling the latest film releases. John Saxe made a deal with Essanay Studios in Chicago for the Milwaukee rights to all its films. The brothers then disengaged themselves from their contract with Hale and remodeled "Scenes of the World" into a 242-seat house called the Theatorium. It was the largest moving picture theater to date in Milwaukee. It had reasonably comfortable seats bolted to the floor, and two large aisles, each with an exit. The outside was embellished with two mythological figures guarding the entrance and a ticket booth shaped like a Moorish minaret. The Theatorium opened each day at noon and presented ten shows, each lasting just under an hour. The program included illustrated songs, a lecture, and several short films, all for five cents.

The theater was crowded at every show, and as Tom Saxe saw to the daily operations, John looked around for a property to develop into another theater. He found an opportunity right across the street at John Callahan's billiard hall. Callahan was a

(continued on page 41)

The Saxe Brothers: Milwaukee's Movie Kings

John and Thomas Saxe were born in 1871 and 1874, respectively, in Newbridge, Ireland. Their family came to America in the early 1880s and settled on a farm near Fox Lake, Wisconsin. By 1889, harsh winters, difficulties of rural life, and poor economic conditions forced the family to relocate to Milwaukee, where the brothers were destined to emerge as the most successful of Milwaukee's early theater operators.

The Saxe family lived in the Merrill Park neighborhood on Thirty-fifth Street just south of Wisconsin Avenue. As preteens, the brothers became newsboys, selling the *Milwaukee Journal* at busy intersections. Their successful sales (and, according to one family legend, their willingness to scrap with other sellers to defend their turf) eventually earned them the highly coveted corner of Third Street and Wisconsin Avenue, to the displeasure of adult sellers. With the profits from years of selling papers, the Saxes ran a small saloon and then a sign painting business. They serviced burlesque theaters, dime museums, opera houses and the legitimate stages, all of which needed new posters and attraction boards painted weekly. After observing the popularity of early motion pictures, they opened several theaters.

The Saxes achieved early success when they

Although they had no experience, John and Thomas Saxe decided to try their hand at running a theater in 1902. They would become two of Milwaukee's most successful movie theater owners. Mary Granberg Collection

showed a film version of *The Passion Play* at the Lyric in March 1908. Even after a two-week run, people were still lined up to see it on the day of the final showing. The film was due to be returned, but Tom Saxe was reluctant to give up such a guaranteed moneymaker. To keep the distributors from getting their film back, he entrusted members of the house orchestra to each take different reels of the film home each night. The film ultimately played an additional fourteen weeks at the Lyric before a court injunction forced the Saxes to surrender the film.

Success followed all of the Saxes' early investments, and in 1908 the brothers incorporated as Saxe Amusement Enterprises. Over the next decade, Saxe AE added the Alhambra, Strand, Miller, and a number of other theaters to its chain. By the 1920s, the company also operated theaters in Green Bay, Waukesha, Beloit, Fond du Lac, Wausau, Madison, Janesville, Neenah, Menasha, Antigo, Marinette, Oshkosh, and Racine.

While Thomas managed the theaters, John Saxe created America's first hamburger chain, the White Tower diners. The brothers eventually located White Towers adjacent to many of their theaters. The Saxe

The Saxe Brothers: Milwaukee's Movie Kings

Veteran theater manager Charles Braun began his career in 1910 booking vaudeville acts into the Majestic, Crystal, and Empress Theaters. From 1918 to 1928, Braun worked for John and Thomas Saxe, managing the Miller on North Third Street. The Saxes breathed new life into the Miller, much as they had with Schlitz's Alhambra. Photo by Albert Kuhli; Sue Braun Collection

The Saxe Brothers: Milwaukee's Movie Kings

(continued from page 39)
brothers also invested in profitable hotels with million-aire Walter Schroeder, including the Retlaw in Fond du Lac and the Schroeder in Milwaukee. For recreation, the brothers took business trips to Hollywood and gambled in Havana. Thomas's daughter, Catherine, said she and her sister Harriet were able to take their friends to the movies any time they wanted, but her father forbade them from having anything to do with the movie business or the people behind the scenes.

Tom Saxe and silent movie star Colleen Moore became good friends, and Moore often visited the Saxe family at their summer home in what is now Trimborn Farm near Greendale. They are pictured during lunch at Gimbel's.
Mary Granberg Collection

On at least one occasion, the entire family accompanied Thomas Saxe on a trip to Hollywood, where they were introduced to dozens of movie stars. "[Silent star] Colleen Moore was a special friend of the family," Catherine said in an interview.

In March 1924, Saxe AE opened its flagship theater, the three-thousand-seat Wisconsin. People could see

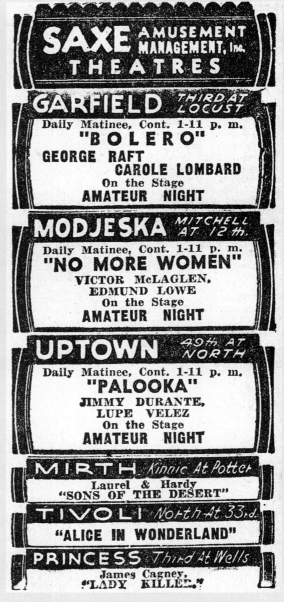

When he returned to the movie business in the 1930s, Thomas Saxe operated a smaller circuit that included these theaters. *Milwaukee Journal*

THE SAXE BROTHERS: MILWAUKEE'S MOVIE KINGS

the seventy-five-foot exterior vertical sign for five miles on a clear night as it flashed the theater's name. Marble staircases, glittering chandeliers, and museum-quality art treasures filled the lobby. The entertainment complex also contained a rooftop dance hall, billiard parlor, bowling alley, and amusement arcade. The following year they rebuilt the Modjeska Theater on Mitchell Street. Once a sister theater to the Princess, the new Modjeska was smaller than the Wisconsin but included many of the same amenities, such as a bowling alley and dance hall.

Next the Saxe brothers opened a series of movie palaces: the Tower, Plaza, Oriental, Uptown, and Garfield. By 1926, Saxe theaters were taking in more than two-thirds of the movie admission dollars in Milwaukee. The following year their Wisconsin theatrical chain comprised more than forty theaters, and the Saxes received several lucrative buyout offers from Universal, Warner, and Paramount, all of which wanted to establish a better foothold in the state. In 1927, Saxe AE finally accepted an offer from a subsidiary of 20th Century Fox and sold its holdings for two million dollars.

Having divested himself of the theater business, Thomas Saxe oversaw his investments in carnival rides, nightclubs, an amusement park, dance halls, a roller rink, parking lots, a Texas fruit farm, apartments, office buildings, houses, and undeveloped lots. His huge farmlands to the south of Milwaukee were purchased and developed as the village of Greendale. Thomas donated other parcels of land to Milwaukee County that became Whitnall Park and Trimborn Farm. In 1933, he returned to the theater business under the name Warner-Saxe Theaters and ran the Parkway, Savoy, Tivoli, Juneau, Lake, Milwaukee, Mirth, Modjeska, and Uptown until his death in 1938. John Saxe, still administering the popular White Tower hamburger restaurants, died the following year.

longtime Wisconsin Avenue pool hall operator who had recently tried to expand his business to include a theater and a penny arcade. Callahan sold his Theater Delight to the Saxe brothers, who completely renovated the hall and named it the Orpheum.

The Orpheum had 340 seats, nearly 100 more than the Theatorium. By playing a different picture at each theater, the Saxes assured themselves of filling both houses. As eager as they were to expand again, the brothers were also extremely shrewd businessmen who avoided the mistake of trying to get too far too fast. Rather than open three or four theaters simultaneously, Tom and John carefully cultivated each new enterprise until it could stand on its own before moving on to the next. In this manner, they steadily built a solid empire of theaters that would make them the force to be reckoned with in Milwaukee's theatrical world.

In late 1907, the Saxes set their sights on a small arcade at Twelfth and Walnut Streets, a bustling district of shops and restaurants. Managed by the elderly Schultz brothers, another team of would-be movie entrepreneurs, the Edison Theater was an outdated penny arcade where patrons activated coin-operated phonographs and

The Saxe brothers remodeled a billiard hall at Second and Wisconsin into their second picture theater, the Orpheum. *Milwaukee Journal Sentinel*

Vitascopes. The Saxes bought the amusement parlor and commissioned architect John Menge Jr. to convert the building into a picture theater, which they named the Globe. The following year the brothers remodeled a storefront at Third Street and Wisconsin Avenue and called it the Lyric.

Next to Wisconsin Avenue, the busiest shopping district in the city was on Mitchell Street, and moving picture houses began to appear there between Sixth and Twelfth Streets. People with no previous experience were leasing storefronts and converting them into theaters. A relatively small investment could purchase projection equipment and seating. Many budding entrepreneurs entered the business with no

In 1910, Mitchell Street was a viable business district, second only to Wisconsin Avenue. UWM Archives, Golda Meir Library

Edward Wagner was one of Milwaukee's motion picture pioneers.
Leona Whitely Collection

more than courage, high hopes, and three hundred dollars. There were a few success stories, but there were many more failures.

Among the early trailblazers on Mitchell Street was Edward Wagner, a restless laborer who saw the movies as a chance to finally go into a business for himself. Wagner and his wife, Martha, opened the Emporium in July 1906, at 626 West Mitchell Street. Shortly after opening, Wagner renamed it the Imperial 5¢ Theater to advertise the price.

Using the Mitchell Street theater as a beginning, Wagner and his family then became involved in running the Happy Hour Theater on Muskego Avenue, the Park Theater on Mitchell Street, and the Wagner Theater on Forest Home Avenue. Wagner stayed in the theater business, running the Garden in South Milwaukee, until his death in 1930.

Not all the pioneers were as lucky as the Wagners. In retrospect, it's easy to see why only innovative and dedicated operators survived. The Dietrich brothers, a trio of piano salesmen, opened the Unique Electric Theater at Tenth and Mitchell Streets in February 1907. The Unique was unique in that it had only seventy-three seats and closed within three months.

Several theaters began to include the term *Electric* after their name so people would instantly know the theater specialized in motion pictures rather than live performances. For a time Milwaukee had the Iola Electric, Union Electric, Trinz Electric, Unique Electric, and Electric Joy.

One of the most successful local motion picture pioneers was Henry Trinz. Trinz

Above: Henry Trinz built up a successful chain of theaters over fifteen years. Edward Trinz Collection

Right: The largest theater in Henry Trinz's chain, the Empire, was financed by the Schlitz Brewing Company. WHS PH 639

and his brothers had operated a saloon in Chicago for Milwaukee's Schlitz Brewery until he moved to Milwaukee early in 1906 and settled near Twelfth and Mitchell Streets. In April, Trinz invested seven hundred dollars to operate a nickel theater at 1202 West Mitchell Street. His success there allowed him to open theaters on Kinnickinnic, Lincoln, and Fond du Lac Avenues that were operated by his brothers Aaron, Samuel, and Joseph. In the summer of 1906, Schlitz invested heavily in the Trinz brothers' Empire Theatre, a large picture and vaudeville house at 1125 West Mitchell Street. Once the Empire was in operation, the brothers bought the former North Side Turn Hall at 1025 West Walnut Street and converted it for motion pictures as the Columbia.

The Trinz chain of theaters grew larger, and by 1914 the brothers were operating the Avenue at Lincoln and Howell Avenues, the Savoy at Twenty-seventh and Center Streets, and the Star at Fifteenth Street and Fond du Lac Avenue in addition to the Columbia and the Empire. In 1920, the Trinz brothers sold their Milwaukee theaters and returned to Chicago, investing their money in a chain of Paramount Theaters.

While Henry Trinz, Edward Wagner, and others were opening their theaters, the

Following the success of their Princess Theater in 1909, the Saxe brothers immediately built an identical theater, the Modjeska, at Twelfth and Mitchell. UWM Archives, Golda Meir Library

Saxe brothers were already moving to the next level. The process of acquiring and renovating small nickelodeons came to an end for the brothers in December 1909, when they opened the magnificent Princess Theater at 738 North Third Street. The next year, Saxe Amusement Enterprises (Saxe AE), as they called their company, opened a sister theater to the Princess at Twelfth and Mitchell Streets. Nearly identical in outward appearance, the new theater was called the Modjeska to honor the great Polish actress Helena Modjeska and the Polish population that lived in the surrounding neighborhood.

The instant acceptance and popularity of the Princess and Modjeska Theaters proved that the upgrading of moving picture theaters appealed to the public. Other

(continued on page 49)

Lady of the Evening: The Princess Theater

In August 1984, a demolition crew punched a hole in the Princess Theater, officially ending the life of one of Milwaukee's oldest movie houses. On the decline since the mid-1950s, the notorious Princess, located at 738 North Third Street, had evolved into an X-rated, unwanted commodity within a downtown district that was in the process of revitalizing itself with new buildings, shopping malls, and skywalks. But few knew the real story behind the Princess, a story that counted some of Milwaukee's most prominent citizens and the president of the United States among its cast of characters.

The property on which the Princess was built originally belonged to Byron Kilbourn, one of the city's founders. In 1897, the Pabst Brewing Company purchased some of the Kilbourn properties, intending to develop these land parcels into restaurants or saloons.

Pabst leased the Third Street land to William L. Kinner, who built a restaurant on the site, but the venture proved unsuccessful and closed in less than a year. The building sat vacant until 1903, when the brewery leased it to a national syndicate that remodeled it into a theater called the Grand. When it opened in May 1904, the Grand featured vaudeville shows four times a day for admission of a dime. The theater prospered, and with the addition of a balcony, seating capacity was increased to nine hundred.

In June 1906 the land and building were included in a sizable transfer of real estate from the Pabst Brewing Company to Clara Schandein Heyl, a great-granddaughter of Pabst patriarch Jacob Best. Clara Heyl later separated from her husband, Jacob Heyl, in a scandalous divorce that held Milwaukee residents' intense interest for more than a year. Following the divorce, Clara took her sons, Reinhard and Helmuth, to live in Berlin, Germany.

In April 1908, the Grand Theater was leased by a national firm that, according to an ad in the *Milwaukee Journal*, showed "moving and talking pictures" and "the human voice pictures." Long-forgotten silent films such as *The Magic of Music* and *The Student's Revenge* were shown, the audio portion provided by a group of actors who huddled behind the screen and shouted out the appropriate lines in time to the actions being shown.

In 1909, the Grand was leased to Tom and John Saxe, who spent fifty thousand dollars to remodel it. The exterior featured a forty-foot facade with an ornamental arch over the entrance and 1,500 incandescent lightbulbs to attract the eye. Inside, plush cushioned seats, a balcony, and four private boxes topped off the brothers' spending spree. On December 16, 1909, the new Princess Theater was formally unveiled to a select audience that included city officials, theater managers, and members of Milwaukee society. Mayor David S. Rose delivered the dedicatory address.

Though the Saxe brothers retained control over the Princess through 1927, ownership of the land came into dispute in the years just following World War I. The Heyl family, still living in Berlin, held the deed to the land. At the outbreak of World War I, Clara's son Helmuth enlisted in the German air force and was quickly promoted to captain. Flying in the squadron of Baron Von Richtofen, Heyl was decorated at the end of the war with the Iron Cross First Class — a decoration from the enemy that the United States government did not take kindly to. In 1921, the federal government seized the Heyls' real estate in Milwaukee under the congressional Trading with the Enemy Act. President Calvin Coolidge issued an executive order allowing the Heyl real estate to be sold. Before a sale could be arranged, however, Helmuth Heyl became a

Lady of the Evening: The Princess Theater

The grand Princess Theater opened its doors in 1909. Here it is as it looked in 1934, under Len Howard's management. Leonard J. Howard Family Collection

United States citizen and was allowed to keep the property upon which the Princess Theater stood. Heyl then settled in upstate New York and acted as a wartime government consultant during World War II. He never returned to Milwaukee.

Len Howard ran the Princess for Fox-Wisconsin beginning in 1933. Howard was promoted in 1944 and moved to Los Angeles, where he managed movie theaters such as the famous Grauman's Chinese during

continued on next page

Lady of the Evening: The Princess Theater

(continued from page 47)

Len Howard and Elvis, during the filming of *Love Me Tender*, circa 1956. Leonard J. Howard Family Collection

the golden age of Hollywood motion picture production with the Fox West Coast Theater chain. Howard then worked in the 20th Century Fox Studios public relations department. In this capacity, he met many of the famous Hollywood stars of the time, including Marilyn Monroe, Jane Russell, Doris Day, Cary Grant, Clark Gable, Robert Wagner, and the up-and-coming Elvis Presley. Howard retired in 1966 and passed away four years later.

In the 1930s, larger, more elaborate movie "palaces" opened around the Princess, and the theater became one of the smaller, less prestigious theaters in the downtown area. By 1943 the Princess was leased by 20th Century Fox studios and showed double-feature B Westerns and action movies. Admission was fifty cents, half of what the larger theaters on Wisconsin Avenue were charging.

As the neighborhood around Third Street began to deteriorate, so did the last vestige of the Princess's integrity and elegance. By 1957 the street-level exterior was drastically altered by the addition of a noncombustible pseudobrick surface. Lost in the conversion were four of the eight doors and the ticket booth, which was moved indoors.

On Thursday, January 14, 1960, the Princess

THE FILM THAT GOES WAY OUT!

From the tops of their heads to the tips of their toes they were

MADE FOR LOVE!!!

ADULTS ONLY— M.P.C.

"The 'D' Girls"

NOW!
CO-FEATURE
The Playboy Girl
ELKE SOMMERS
"SWEET ECSTACY"
PRINCESS
N. 3rd and Wisconsin
OPEN DAILY 9 A.M.

By 1960, the Princess, billing itself as a "fine arts theater," began to show adult-themed films. *Milwaukee Journal*

showed its last legitimate film, *The Five Pennies*, starring Danny Kaye and Louis Armstrong. The following day, the *Milwaukee Journal* and *Sentinel* carried large advertisements for films at the Princess that were "frank and daring" and "for adults only." The sensational promotion for these films attracted a different kind of theatergoer. In the early 1960s, the Princess was the place in Milwaukee to see the new Brigitte Bardot films; the 1970s saw a more explicit version of adult movies at the theater.

In 1984, ownership of the Princess transferred to yet another generation of Heyl heirs when Helmuth died at age seventy-eight in New York. His family had owned the land for eighty-seven years. On March 9, 1984, the Milwaukee Redevelopment Authority revealed it was buying the building and land for $292,113 as part of a larger revitalization project.

On Saturday evening, August 11, the Princess showed its last film, *Sex Games*, and closed its doors, without fanfare, for the final time. Admission during the last years had been five dollars, making it the most expensive motion picture theater in Milwaukee at the time. Demolition crews began to raze the theater at 12:00 p.m., Friday, August 31, 1984, making a quick end to the theater that was billed on its opening night in 1909 as "The Coziest Little Theater in the West."

exhibitors soon realized that the storefront nickelodeons were doomed, and they could either follow the trend toward bigger and better houses or fall by the wayside. There was no more room for naive investors possessing only determination and a white sheet for a screen.

By 1910, Milwaukee had sixty-four operating movie theaters. Even as they increased in popularity, antitheater sentiment began to grow. Reformers, social workers, and church groups feared theaters and the pictures they showed would lead to the country's moral decay. There was a nationwide movement to censor the theaters, and a "Closed Sunday" law went on the books in major cities across the United States. This law prohibited any form of entertainment on Sundays, including vaudeville, operatic concerts, motion picture showings at the YMCA, and even scholarly lectures. Raids did occur around the city, and anyone present was likely to be arrested.

Another example of this "blue law" movement in Milwaukee was a neighborhood petition circulated in 1910 to prohibit the licensing of a new nickel theater on the corner of South Eighth and Mitchell Streets. The petition, signed by twenty-one area residents, asked that building inspector Edward Koch deny the theater a license on the grounds that it would be a nuisance on the primarily residential street. Despite the opposition, the Central Theater was granted its license and remained in business until 1952 under such names as the Midget and the Popularity before closing as the Delta Theater.

Even with growing criticism, it was not until 1911 that Milwaukee passed ordinances and zoning regulations specifically for motion picture theaters. The first action was to regulate the operation of film projectors as well as the construction, alteration, or remodeling of any building intended for use as a moving picture theater. In 1912, a new division was organized in the City Inspection Office for the sole purpose of theater inspection. Those theaters that did not conform to the new city codes were fined or closed altogether. The city also passed ordinances and regulations concerning the handling and storage of the dangerously flammable nitrate film.

Show business veteran Otto Meister had been exhibiting pictures at his Vaudette Theater on North Third Street since 1908 and was netting about nineteen thousand dollars a year for his efforts. He had been watching the crowds at the Princess across the street for some time, all the while planning a defensive move. Meister formed the Central Amusement Company with John Freuler in the spring of 1911, and the two concocted a theater for moving pictures, the likes of which existed only in someone's wildest dreams. Meister held a ninety-nine-year lease on the land at 212 West Wisconsin Avenue, and he proceeded to tear down the building that in the late 1890s had housed his Nickelodeon and Phanta-Phone Theaters. Construction of the

The Butterfly Theater, located at 212 West Wisconsin Avenue, was a sight to behold. Early advertisements proclaimed it to be "Milwaukee's movie palace." The Butterfly was in operation from 1911 to 1930. Jessie Walker Collection

Meister/Freuler theater, to be called the Butterfly, began in June 1911 and was completed by the end of August.

On September 2, the doors of the outrageously elegant Butterfly Theater opened to great public acclaim. With fifteen hundred seats, walls swathed in plush red velvet, and a proscenium done up in gold and silver leaf, the interior of the Butterfly was an amazing amalgamation. Canaries in gilded cages chirped in the lobby as patrons passed to the auditorium. But the real attraction was the theater's namesake, a huge terra cotta butterfly with a human body that rested on the exterior facade. The spectacular piece measured twenty-seven feet from wing tip to wing tip and was illuminated by a thousand lightbulbs. An additional two thousand bulbs graced the remainder of the facade.

The Butterfly boasted a ten-piece house orchestra, a pipe organ that cost ten thousand dollars, and six classically trained opera singers. The ventilation system was promoted as the most modern available and was capable of completely changing the air in the auditorium every three minutes. In addition, Meister and Freuler claimed that their theater was "absolutely fireproof."

Meister, presiding over the opening of the Butterfly like a proud father, reached back to his dime museum days and resurrected his 1895 slogan from the Wonderland. The inaugural advertisement for Meister's Butterfly boasted, "A dollar show for a dime."

The opening-night program featured "pictures never before shown in the United States" as well as "side-splitting comedies" and "realistic photo-dramas." If Milwaukee's nickelodeon era suffered a crippling blow with the opening of the Princess, then it surely died on September 2, 1911, at the premiere of the Butterfly. Nickel admissions and storefront theaters would now become a thing of the past. The newer, more elegant theaters were being referred to as "photoplay houses," reflecting the quality of the theater and the new idea of longer films, or photoplays, that told complete stories.

THREE
The Photoplay Houses: 1912–1923

"We didn't need dialogue. We had faces."—Norma Desmond (Gloria Swanson), Sunset Boulevard

The Princess and Butterfly Theaters represented a new trend in moving picture houses. Products of the reform movement led by citizens, civic leaders, and clergy to improve theater conditions (or force them to close), they were designed to attract a more affluent clientele. Their luxurious decor, balconies, and box seats had previously been reserved for the legitimate stages.

NORTH SIDE MOVING PICTURE THEATER IS SAFE FROM FIRE

An extremely rare photo of one of Milwaukee's first motion picture theaters, the Olympic Theater at Seventh and Walnut. The theater was closed by 1917.
Milwaukee Sentinel

But Milwaukee's theater owners wanted to legitimize their businesses further. A *Milwaukee Journal* article on June 13, 1911, explained that a chief criticism of moving picture shows of the past had been that their darkness "gave opportunity for flirtations leading to undesirable acquaintances on the part of young girls and boys." Now the problem of a totally darkened theater was alleviated in part by technological advancements, such as specially designed screens and projectors with increased illumination. In addition, a Milwaukee city ordinance published in June 1911 outlined new regulations for proper lighting, ventilation, exits, and fireproofing of movie theaters. Those who did not comply with the ordinance could be fined up to one hundred dollars or sentenced to up to sixty days' imprisonment.

To promote their businesses and police their industry, the city's showmen formed the Exhibitors' League of Milwaukee. John Freuler was the league's first president and served until 1916, when he was replaced by Henry Trinz. Under Freuler's lead-

In 1911, the Alhambra (here advertising the feature *Swim Girl Swim*) was Milwaukee's largest motion picture theater. By the 1920s, it was nearly obsolete.
Dave Prentice Collection

ership, the Exhibitors' League enhanced the image of its theaters by voluntarily exceeding the city's guidelines. League treasurer Thomas Saxe said, "If a girl is insulted, the police are called and it hurts every moving picture show in the city. There is not a motion picture man in this city who can afford to allow such a thing to happen." League members now employed responsible elderly men as doorkeepers and ushers to assure adequate protection for young ladies. These efforts, along with the elegance of the new photoplay houses, brought newfound respectability to motion pictures.

With continually increasing attendance and their future in the industry now appearing secure, Saxe AE had its eyes on the venerable Alhambra Theater at Fourth and Wisconsin. The former vaudeville house had been converted from a legitimate stage into an all-movie theater in 1911.

The Alhambra had been designed for the Schlitz Brewery by Charles Kirchhoff and had opened in December 1896. Opening night at this French-inspired palace,

The Saxe brothers leased the unprofitable Alhambra vaudeville theater from Schlitz Brewery in 1911 and turned it into a highly profitable motion picture theater. For a time, the Alhambra was recognized as the largest motion picture theater in the world.
Larry Widen Collection

constructed at a cost of more than half a million dollars, saw overflow crowds gasping at the four thousand electric lights, private boxes, and plush red velvet draperies. Police were called to help turn away the hundreds who could not get in as Schlitz owners Henry, Alfred, and August Uihlein sat in their private box at stage left and watched eleven acts of the highest-class vaudeville.

The Alhambra operated in the black for the next decade under the capable management of Oscar Miller. Although Miller was involved financially in various amusement enterprises, such as the Palace Dime Museum on Third Street and the Coney Island summer park in Shorewood, his first allegiance was to the Alhambra, and he personally selected all of the acts that played there. When Miller died unexpectedly in 1905, the Alhambra, without competent management, foundered for several years.

By 1911, Herman Fehr, the Alhambra's acting manager and one of the owners, feared that Schlitz would have to sell the theater. By chance, Fehr made the acquaintance of Samuel Rothapfel while riding a train to Milwaukee. Rothapfel (who was better known as "Roxy" and who would go on to open the renowned Roxy Theater in New York) was fast becoming a legend in theatrical circles for his ability to breathe new life into dying theaters. Fehr hired Roxy on the spot to save the Alhambra. Roxy arrived in June and advised Fehr to show motion pictures at the Alhambra. Under Roxy's supervision, the three-thousand-seat theater became for a time the largest moving picture house in the world.

Roxy installed a nursery for the convenience of matinee-going mothers, hired a staff of ushers, installed a projection booth, ordered new carpets and draperies, and covered the orchestra pit. As his final public relations master stroke, Roxy contacted one thousand prominent citizens with this letter:

> Enclosed please find two tickets for the new Alhambra theater, which will admit yourself and a friend to see the beautiful new theater and the wonderful Italian production, "The Fall of Troy," which cost the producers more than $30,000. Please do not feel that you are obligated to the theater in any way. We merely wish to show you what remarkable advances have been made in motion photography and what a valuable adjunct the moving picture has become as an educator.—Respectfully yours, S. L. Rothapfel

The Alhambra began its new programming in the summer of 1911, and the Saxe brothers, lured by the theater's substantial profits, quickly offered forty thousand dollars to lease the Alhambra. They won the lease and now controlled eight theaters: the Juneau, Globe, Princess, Orpheum, Theatorium, Modjeska, Crystal, and Alhambra.

As 1912 began, the public was demanding upscale theaters with many amenities, and the city's movie exhibitors temporarily stopped expanding, instead working to solidify their current positions. The Trinz family still controlled the Columbia, Empire, Avenue, and Savoy, as well as a recent addition, the Rainbow Theater at Twenty-seventh Street and Lisbon Avenue. Edward Wagner was working to spruce up his recent acquisitions in Hartford, Racine, and Waukesha in addition to his Milwaukee theaters. John Freuler and Otto Meister, through their Central Amusement Company, controlled the Butterfly and the Vaudette, as well as the Atlas Theater at Third Street and North Avenue and the Climax Theater at Twentieth Street and Fond du Lac Avenue. Many former nickelodeon operators who had not upgraded their theaters were either working for someone else or out of the business.

The construction of a competitive theater was now so expensive that many operators looking to build sought the financial assistance of large local companies, such as the breweries. The Schlitz interests knew the advantages of investing in a theater; they had financed the Empire at Twelfth and Mitchell Streets and the New Star on North Third Street. Miller Brewery had already invested in the Juneau at Sixth and Mitchell Streets and was constructing the Strand, a $200,000 theater/office/storefront on Wisconsin Avenue near Fifth Street.

The Strand advertised two thousand seats "for perfect comfort" and the latest projection equipment that produced "pictures without a flicker" and assured "perfect ease on the eyes and nervous system." The theater also featured a ventilation system that guaranteed that the "last audience of the night will be assured as spring-like

Above: The Palace Theater on Sixth and Wisconsin was the local link in the powerful RKO vaudeville circuit. *Milwaukee Journal Sentinel*

Right: The White House opened in December 1916. *Evening Wisconsin*

an atmosphere as the first audience in the morning." To alleviate fears of a fire panic, a sufficient number of exits were included in the plans so that the entire house could be cleared in one minute without disorder.

Miller Brewery soon turned the management of the Strand over to Saxe AE and began to plan its next investment. The brewery owned a large parcel of land on the west side of Third Street just north of Wisconsin Avenue. Frederick Miller had purchased the land in 1910, but the brewery didn't develop it until 1917, when it opened the Miller Theater. Mayor Daniel W. Hoan gave a dedicatory speech at the opening and announced that Saxe AE would be managing the Miller, "Milwaukee's newest recreation palace."

While Miller was working on its theaters, the Joseph Schlitz Brewing Company began development of a new vaudeville and picture theater at Sixth Street and Wisconsin Avenue. Local architects Charles Kirchhoff and Thomas Rose drew up plans in 1915 for a $350,000 theater/office building that became known as the Palace. Although Schlitz intended the 2,400-seat house to be a live stage theater, it remained so for only a dozen years before converting to motion pictures.

Faced with a flurry of theaters opening under their noses, Otto Meister and John Freuler decided to erect another house on Third Street, on the lot directly adjacent to the Vaudette Theater. They demolished the old Wonderland Scenic Theater on the site and hired architect Henry Lotter to design a new and unique theater. Meister's experience in the dime museums taught him that gimmicks sold tickets, and Lotter came up with an innovative concept that called for the new theater's auditorium to

White House Theater
"THE HOUSE THAT'S DIFFERENT"
Third St., between Grand Ave. and Wells St.
OPENS TODAY 1 P. M.
CHANGE OF PROGRAM DAILY
5c—ADMISSION—5c RESERVED SECTION 10c

be reversed. When the customer walked in, instead of facing the screen, he would have his back to it. Originally planning to call his theater the Capitol, Meister changed the name at the last minute to the White House and advertised it as "The House That's Different."

The White House, located on the west side of North Third Street, was popular from 1917 until its demise in the mid-1950s. The unusual White House was the brainchild of owner Otto Meister, a local show biz legend. Meister's creativity, as seen here in his display promoting *Around the World in 18 Days,* made him a legend in Hollywood at several of the studios. Meister died in 1944 after spending more than a half century in show business. Photo by Louis Kuhli

The planning and execution of the White House took longer and cost more than either Meister or Freuler had counted on, and to raise emergency cash, they sold the Butterfly Theater but retained their ninety-nine-year lease on the land. With funds from the sale of the Butterfly, they completed the White House, and it opened for business on December 16, 1916. Over the years the theater gained a reputation as Milwaukee's "flip-flop theater," and Meister was on the job there every day until his death in July 1944.

Throughout the 1910s, the popularity of the movies snowballed. Films and their

(continued on page 61)

The Top Stars of Silent Films

Roscoe "Fatty" Arbuckle, 1887–1933

Fatty Arbuckle began his career with the Chicago-based Selig Polyscope Film Company in 1908. Mack Sennett discovered him and asked him to join the Keystone Kops comedies. Despite his girth (he was 5'10" and weighed in at 300 pounds), Arbuckle was surprisingly agile. His early comedies were fast-paced and full of chase scenes and sight gags. Arbuckle pioneered the famous "pie in the face," a classic element of silent film comedy. At the height of his career, he earned the astronomical sum of one million dollars a year. In 1921, Arbuckle held a party in a San Francisco hotel room, where a young woman later died. Although Arbuckle was eventually acquitted of her murder, his career was ruined. Many film historians have called his story one of the great tragedies of Hollywood.

Wisconsin Center for Film and Theater Research, Name File Stills

Theda Bara, 1885–1955

Theda Bara, billed as "the Vamp," was one of the most popular screen actresses, and the first sex symbol, of the time. Bara made more than forty feature films beginning in 1914, often appearing in risqué costumes that left little to the imagination. In 1926, Bara retired, spending the remainder of her life in Hollywood and Cincinnati.

Clara Bow, 1905–1965

Clara Bow was best known for her roles as a liberated woman of the 1920s. She made fifty-eight films in a career that lasted just eleven years. In 1927, Bow starred in *Wings*, a war picture that won the first Best Picture Academy Award. After movies began to utilize sound, Bow's career declined, partly because of her thick Brooklyn accent.

Louise Brooks, 1906–1985

Louise Brooks began her career as a dancer in the Ziegfeld Follies on Broadway, where she was noticed by a Paramount Pictures scout for her great beauty. Soon she was playing the lead female role in comedies and flapper films. Her pageboy haircut started a trend among American women.

Wisconsin Center for Film and Theater Research, Name File Stills

Charlie Chaplin, 1889–1977

An actor, director, writer, and producer, Charlie Chaplin emerged as one of the most creative stars of the silent film era. The English-born Chaplin first performed in a music hall at the age of five, and in his early twenties he toured the United States with a comedy troupe. Chaplin stayed on when the troupe returned to England, and Keystone Film Company producer Mack Sennett hired him. Chaplin quickly became adept at film acting. He developed his famous Little Tramp persona and became Keystone's top star. Chaplin formed

The Top Stars of Silent Films

United Artists in 1919 with partners Mary Pickford, Douglas Fairbanks, and D. W. Griffith.

Douglas Fairbanks, 1883–1939

Douglas Fairbanks performed on the Denver stage before moving to New York in 1900 to pursue an acting career. He worked in a hardware store and as a clerk in a Wall Street office before his Broadway debut in 1902. Fairbanks joined Triangle Pictures in 1914 and there began working with D. W. Griffith. He met Mary Pickford at a party in 1916, and they began a relationship. In 1920, Fairbanks, the veteran of thirty romantic comedies, took a chance with the action film *The Mark of Zorro*. The picture was a smash success, and Fairbanks became one of the biggest stars in the history of cinema.

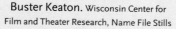

Buster Keaton. Wisconsin Center for Film and Theater Research, Name File Stills

Lillian Gish (Lillian de Guiche), 1893–1993

In 1914, Mary Pickford met Lillian Gish and her sister, Dorothy, and got them acting jobs with Biograph Studios, working in D. W. Griffith's films. Lillian became a major silent film star, becoming known as "the First Lady of the Silent Screen." Preferring silent movies, she chose not to appear in talking pictures. Instead, she acted on the stage for the most part in the 1930s and early 1940s. Returning to movies in the 1940s, Gish was nominated for Best Supporting Actress for her work in 1946's *Duel in the Sun*. Her last screen appearance was in the 1987 film *The Whales of August*, at the age of ninety-three, with veteran actresses Bette Davis and Ann Sothern.

Buster Keaton, 1895–1966

At the age of three, Buster Keaton began performing with his parents as the Three Keatons. In 1917, Keaton met Fatty Arbuckle in New York City and was hired as a costar and gagman. He went on to make 127 films and enjoyed the peak of his popularity from 1920 to 1932. Keaton spent most of the 1930s in obscurity, working as a writer for the Marx Brothers and Red Skelton. He made cameo appearances in several later films, most notably *Sunset Boulevard* in 1950 and *It's a Mad, Mad, Mad, Mad World* in 1963.

Harold Lloyd, 1893–1971

Harold Lloyd ranks alongside Charlie Chaplin and Buster Keaton as one of the most popular and influential film comedians of the silent film era. He made nearly two hundred films, both silent and sound, between 1914 and 1947. Lloyd's films usually contained an extended chase scene or a daredevil physical feat, such as hanging from the hands of a clock high above the street.

Mary Miles Minter, 1902–1984

Mary Minter, at age twenty, was the star of more than fifty films when her career was destroyed by a sensational scandal involving the murder of her lover, forty-nine-year-old director William Desmond Taylor. The public no longer accepted her as the demure girl next door in films, and she was fired by her studio. Minter left Hollywood and lived the rest of her life in obscurity in Santa Monica until her death at age eighty-two.

(continued on next page)

The Top Stars of Silent Films

(continued from page 59)

Colleen Moore, 1900–1988

Colleen Moore's first major success was the 1923 film *Flaming Youth*. Her vivacious portrayal of a liberated

From an ad for Saxe theaters, circa 1927. *Milwaukee Sentinel*

flapper girl made her one of the most talked about actresses of her day. Along with Louise Brooks, Moore epitomized young-adult society of the 1920s. Her bobbed hairstyle was widely copied throughout the world. By 1935,

however, Moore could no longer play the ingénue, and she walked away from her film career a wealthy woman.

Jack Pickford, 1896–1933

The brother of actress Mary Pickford, Jack Pickford was only fourteen when Biograph Studios signed him to perform in motion pictures. When his sister signed a contract for one million dollars with First National Pictures, Jack got a lucrative deal as well. Despite his on-screen image as the boy next door, Pickford's private life was ravaged by severe alcoholism and the syphilis that would eventually kill him. He appeared in more than seventy films before his death at age thirty-six.

Mary Pickford, 1892–1979

D. W. Griffith screen-tested and hired Mary Pickford for a part in a one-reel thriller, *The Lonely Villa*, in 1909. Pickford would go on to become Hollywood's biggest female star, the first female actor to receive more than a million dollars per year, and one of the few stars to prove successful in both the silent film era and the sound film period. She won the 1929 Best Actress Academy Award for her role in *Coquette* but retired from films four years later, after a series of disappointing roles and the public's inability to accept Pickford in roles that reflected her own age, rather than teenage heroines.

Rudolph Valentino, 1895–1926

A classically trained dancer, Rudolph Valentino had earned small parts in several films by 1920. He be-

Wisconsin Center for Film and Theater Research, Name File Stills

came a star with *The Four Horsemen of the Apocalypse* and *The Sheik*, both released in 1921. An estimated 100,000 people lined the streets of New York to pay their respects at his funeral in 1926.

SECOND STREET NEAR GRAND AV.
OLINGER'S
PARADISE
OPEN TODAY
MARY PICKFORD
in "THE ETERNAL GRIND," and
Charlie Chaplin
in "THE CHAMPION."
Double Headline Features for Only
TEN CENTS.
Continuous Show 11 A. M. to 11 P. M.

Paradise Theater ad,
1916. *Milwaukee Sentinel*

audiences were becoming more sophisticated, and subjects ranged from comedy to Cleopatra. Movie stars became household names, and personalities such as Mary Pickford, Charlie Chaplin, Gloria Swanson, and Lillian Gish enjoyed fame and wealth. Chaplin and Swanson were two stars whom John Freuler discovered and signed to make pictures for his Mutual Films. In 1916, Freuler outbid Paramount, Universal, and other studios for the services of Charlie Chaplin. Freuler paid $670,000 to Chaplin in a precedent-setting deal that would eventually become standard within the industry.

Trendy subjects included the Keystone Film Company's riotous slapstick humor. Also popular was the weekly serial, with a new "cliff-hanger" arriving each week at the theaters to keep audiences on the edge of their seats. The American landscape proved to be a ready-made set for Western films, and the popular horror film genre can also trace its roots to this age of moviemaking.

In Milwaukee, Otto Meister was creating a trend of his own, with clever advertising and displays for the Mack Sennett comedies that played at the Vaudette and White House. He was famous for decorating the outside of his theaters with elaborate displays and gimmicks to call attention to the shows. Word of Meister's extraordinary success soon reached Hollywood, and he became a hero to Sennett and his repertory company. When Meister visited the movie capital in 1917, Sennett featured Meister in a comedy called *Droppington's Family Tree*. Projectionist Walter Plato, who first worked at the White House in 1931, said that Meister was a genius when it came to promotion and advertising, always decorating the front of the theater with posters and other attention-getting devices. At the time, the White House showed mostly Westerns, and Meister liked to change films four or five times a week, sometimes to the consternation of his projectionists. "There'd be days when you'd have a couple dozen reels coming in and going out . . . that made for some gray hairs," Plato said.

To go along with the more elaborate movie houses, as early as the 1910s major film studios began to produce movies that cost $100,000 and reaped more than ten times that amount in profits. John Freuler's Mutual Films was one of the original investors in *The Birth of a Nation*, which opened in 1915 to public acclaim. During the

Important Films of the Silent Era

As movies gained popularity, filmmakers moved away from capturing events, such as a sneeze or a chase, and began to tell stories. The early silent film stories, like the French film *A Trip to the Moon* (1902) by George Melies or *The Great Train Robbery* (1903) by Edwin S. Porter, are good examples of how the new medium was growing. But it wasn't until 1915, with D. W. Griffith's epic *The Birth of a Nation*, that the full extent of film's storytelling power was realized. Griffith's use of close-ups and other camera techniques ushered in a new era of cinema. Most important, at nearly three hours, *The Birth of a Nation* showed that a full-length film could hold an audience's attention. These were some of the other films that thrilled movie-goers in the years before talking pictures:

Intolerance (1916)

Stars: Lillian Gish, Mae Marsh, Bessie Love, Tod Browning, Monte Blue, Alma Rubens, Douglas Fairbanks (uncredited). Director: D. W. Griffith.

Intolerance was an expensive undertaking, with monumental sets, lavish period costumes and more than three thousand extras. Four parallel storylines depicted human intolerance over three thousand years. The film cost about two million dollars to make (around forty million in 2005 dollars), an astronomical sum in 1916. Griffith's ego overshadowed sound financial judgment, and when the film performed poorly at the box office, it caused Triangle Pictures to go bankrupt.

Broken Blossoms (1919)

Stars: Lillian Gish, Richard Barthelmess, Donald Crisp. Director: D. W. Griffith.

Broken Blossoms is the story of a Chinese man living in England. When he falls in love with an English woman, he incurs the wrath of the townspeople who disapprove of the interracial romance. On the other side of the camera, Griffith played it safe by casting a Caucasian actor, Richard Barthelmess, in the role of the Chinese man.

Four Horsemen of the Apocalypse (1921)

Star: Rudolph Valentino. Director: Rex Ingram.

With its depiction of the devastated French countryside, *The Four Horsemen of the Apocalypse* is one the first antiwar films ever made. It was one of the top-grossing silent films of all time and launched the career of Rudolph Valentino, who would go on to become one of the biggest stars of the silent film era.

The Sheik (1921)

Star: Rudolph Valentino. Director: George Wynn.

The Sheik was not a great artistic achievement, but it was a huge hit with women who swooned over the handsome Valentino. A 1926 sequel, *The Son of the Sheik*, was completed just before Valentino's untimely death.

Safety Last (1923)

Star: Harold Lloyd. Director: Fred C. Newmeyer.

Harold Lloyd hanging from the hands of a clock high above the street for the film *Safety Last* is one of the most famous images in all of cinema. Lloyd did many of these dangerous stunts himself, despite having only three fingers on his right hand, the result of a 1919 accident with a prop bomb.

Important Films of the Silent Era

The Phantom of the Opera (1925)

Stars: Lon Chaney, Mary Philbin, Norman Kerry. Director: Rupert Julian.

The story of a disfigured phantom who haunts the Paris Opera House still makes an impression eighty years after its release. This first film version is justifiably famous for Chaney's horrific, self-applied makeup, which was kept hidden from the press until the film's premiere. The success of *The Phantom* established Universal Studios as the industry leader in horror films for decades to come.

It (1927)

Star: Clara Bow. Director: Clarence G. Badger.

With the release of this film, Clara Bow became known as the "It" girl, "it" being a euphemism for sexual charisma. Risqué in its day, the story centers around a shop girl who sets her sights on the handsome owner. Her plans backfire when a reporter writes a story claiming she is an unwed mother.

The General (1927)

Star: Buster Keaton. Directors: Clyde Bruckman, Buster Keaton.

In *The General*, Keaton performed dangerous physical stunts on and around a moving train, which included jumping from the engine to a boxcar, sitting on the cowcatcher, and running along the roof. The climax of the film includes one of the most expensive shots in motion picture history up to that time, a spectacular scene where a bridge collapses as a railroad train crosses it.

Wings (1927)

Stars: Charles "Buddy" Rogers, Richard Arlen, Clara Bow, Gary Cooper. Director: William A. Wellman.

In this film, which won the first Best Picture Academy Award in 1929, World War I fighter pilots become enamored with the same girl, resulting in a competition that threatens their friendship.

premiere run, the film grossed more than fifteen million dollars, partly due to the inflated admission price of two dollars per seat. *The Birth of a Nation* made even the harshest critics of moving pictures admit that Griffith's masterful direction helped movies evolve into an important art form.

Local businesses continued to invest in places to show this growing art form. In 1921, Schlitz Brewing Company hired architects Kirchhoff and Rose to revamp the brewery's Palm Garden at Third and Wisconsin. Originally designed by Kirchhoff in 1895, the spectacularly arched structure was one of Milwaukee's favorite restaurants and night spots. The garden was a reproduction of the beer gardens and halls popular in 1890s Germany. Schlitz beer was the only beverage sold at the Palm Garden, and it was a popular place to have lunch or listen to one of the city's orchestras.

The Cost of Early Films

1903	*The Great Train Robbery* (directed by Edwin S. Porter)	$150
1913	*Judith of Bethulia* (directed by D. W. Griffith)	$36,000
1915	*The Birth of a Nation* (directed by D. W. Griffith)	$110,000
1916	*Intolerance* (directed by D. W. Griffith)	$1,900,000
1920	*Way Down East* (directed by D. W. Griffith)	$175,000
1923	*The Ten Commandments* (directed by Cecil B. DeMille)	$1,300,000
1925	*The Phantom of the Opera* (directed by Rupert Julian)	$635,000
1926	*Ben-Hur: A Tale of the Christ* (directed by Fred C. Niblo)	$4,000,000
1927	*The Jazz Singer* (directed by Alan Crosland)	$500,000
1931	*The Public Enemy* (directed by William A. Wellman)	$150,000
1933	*King Kong* (directed by Merian C. Cooper, Ernest B. Schoedsack)	$672,000
1936	*Modern Times* (directed by Charles Chaplin)	$1,500,000
1937	*Snow White and the Seven Dwarfs* (directed by Walt Disney)	$1,700,000
1939	*Gone with the Wind* (directed by Victor Fleming)	$4,250,000
1941	*Citizen Kane* (directed by Orson Welles)	$3,000,000

The enactment of Prohibition in 1920 delivered the death blow to the Palm Garden, but rather than lose the income from this prime piece of real estate at the city's busiest intersection, the brewery again commissioned Kirchhoff and Rose to convert the Palm Garden into a motion picture theater. They removed the potted palm trees and covered the exquisite murals. Permanent seats were fixed to the floor, the entrance of hand-carved wood was replaced, and downtown Milwaukee had another theater, the Garden. With 1,250 seats in the new Garden, 2,400 in the Palace, 2,000 in the Strand, and 3,000 in the Alhambra, the once-majestic 900-seat Princess was now one of the smallest of the downtown theaters, just thirteen years after it had been the largest.

The movement to see who could build the biggest and best picture theater had reached full steam. In 1924, the Saxe brothers astounded everyone with the opening of Milwaukee's first movie "palace."

Above: The nineteenth-century Schlitz Palm Garden was renovated into the Garden Motion Picture Theater in 1921. *Larry Widen Collection*

Left: In order to make big-budget pictures profitable, Hollywood studios often played them at only one location and sold reserve tickets. *Ben-Hur* played at the Strand for almost a year. *Milwaukee Sentinel*

FOUR

THE MOVIE PALACES: 1924–1931

"Adding sound to movies would be like putting lipstick on the Venus de Milo."
—Mary Pickford

In 1923 Saxe Amusement Enterprises made a bold move to stay ahead of the increasing competition. The brothers commissioned the internationally renowned architectural firm of C. W. and George Rapp to design a "palace" for motion pictures. Located at Sixth and Wisconsin, the new Saxe theater, aptly named the Wisconsin, opened during a March blizzard in 1924. The theater, the twenty-eighth in their chain, was built as part of the larger Carpenter Building and had a price tag of two million dollars. In spite of the weather, two thousand people lined Wisconsin Avenue to be part of the first audience. A seventy-five-voice choir, an orchestra performance, an organ duo, a newsreel, a Miss Wisconsin Theater beauty contest, films, and a parade from the Pfister Hotel were all part of opening-day festivities.

The debut of the Wisconsin ushered in the golden age of the movie palace in Milwaukee. What set this new breed of theaters apart was their size as well as their specialized themes. The Wisconsin and the movie palaces that followed it were designed with special motifs that enhanced the romantic images Hollywood placed on the screen. In front of the Wisconsin, a spectacular seventy-five-foot vertical sign could be seen for miles. With its French baroque interior, marble grand staircase, and elegant chandeliers, the Wisconsin set a benchmark for the Saxe brothers' rivals.

The opening of Saxe's Wisconsin set off a chain reaction. Rival exhibitors obtained financial backing and hired architects and builders to create theaters in a similar vein. Although the new palaces that followed promised increased profits to

When it opened in 1924, Saxe's opulent Wisconsin Theater seated nearly 3,000 people. Theatergoers attending Milwaukee's first true movie "palace" entered through a white marble lobby with a grand staircase that led to the mezzanine and balcony. Three large chandeliers lent an elegant glow to the lobby's heavily gilded ornamentation.
Photo by Albert Kuhli

The foyer at Milwaukee's Palace led to a Beaux Arts–style theater designed by the local firm Kirchoff and Rose.
Theatre Historical Society of America

Competition to fill seats each night continued to escalate, and theater owners learned that seating the moviegoer in splendid surroundings went a long way toward assuring a full house. Often, the title of the feature was lost in the advertisements that proclaimed the glowing attributes of the theater in which it was shown.
Milwaukee Sentinel

exhibitors, these theaters held even more significance for patrons. The stylistic themes were designed to transport theatergoers to exotic and beautiful settings. In addition, all customers, whether rich or poor, were treated with regal grace by a staff of highly trained ushers. A doorman, someone to take coats, and ushers to assist in locating "the best remaining seats" were common fixtures. Going to the movies became an experience in splendor. In a day when traveling was a pastime reserved for the rich, the common man could pay thirty-five cents and spend three hours in a facsimile of a Viennese opera house, a French palace, or a Venetian garden. Hollywood stars were idols, and the palaces that housed them provided escape from jobs, money troubles, and other pressures of life. With their plush decors, ornate plasterwork, subtle lighting, and elegant themes, these new movie palaces exceeded the standards set by even the elegant legitimate stages.

Some of the most memorable theaters constructed during this time included the Egyptian, Venetian, Avalon, Zenith, and National, which were designed in the "atmospheric" style that came into

Downtown movie palaces had a full staff of ushers and service people to attend to every patron's needs. While the films ran, staff polished brass, cleaned carpets, and freshened restrooms.
Photo by Albert Kuhli

prominence during the late 1920s. Atmospheric movie palaces were first designed in Texas by architect John Eberson, whose creations gave patrons the illusion of sitting in an open-air courtyard at dusk. The auditorium walls rose into a blue-domed ceiling twinkling with stars that were actually fashioned from recessed lightbulbs of various colors. The atmospheric theaters featured trees, vegetation, and ivy hanging from balconies, with arcade walks to complete the fantasy setting.

Architectural Details of Movie Palaces

The Venetian (1927)

As its name implied, the Venetian boasted an Italian Renaissance decor. Sculptural details in the theater's lobby depicted gaines, female figures serving as ornamental support in place of columns or pillars. Gaines, which originally appeared in Egyptian and Greek architecture, were used prominently during the Renaissance and in the classic revival of the nineteenth century.

This figural decoration from the Venetian Theater was one of six that flanked the lobby. Photo by Larry Widen

The Warner/Grand (1931)

The Warner/Grand was characterized by two distinctive styles. The theater's lobby was art deco style with its emphasis on geometric simplicity. By contrast,

Top: This three-by-three-inch ceramic tile illustrates the art deco style in the Warner Theater's lobby. Photo by Larry Widen

Above: Mural in the Warner balcony. Photo by Larry Widen

the auditorium was adorned in the French Renaissance style and included velvet-draped murals that portrayed members of the eighteenth-century aristocracy, rich fabrics, and two-handled ceramic vases decorated with mythological characters.

The Egyptian (1926)

The Egyptian drew its aesthetic inspiration from ancient Egypt. Scarabs, winged sun disks, lotus buds, and six eighteen-foot-tall male figures, modeled after the colossi of Osiris in the Temple of Luxor, graced the interior in a palette of gold, ruby red, teal blue, and Nile green. In addition, the red and black leather seats included ebony arm-rests and illuminated iron seat ends depicting a pharaoh's face.

Seat ends in the Egyptian Theater depicted a pharaoh's face. Photo by Larry Widen

The Uptown (1926)

The art deco movement was a new phenomenon when the Uptown Theater opened on Milwaukee's north side in 1926, just one year after the Exposition des Arts Décoratifs et Industriels Modernes in Paris from which the movement drew its name. One of the inspirations of the movement, Native American art, could be seen in the Uptown's blue glazed tiles, which evoked a Navajo directional motif. These tiles were used in a fountain in the theater's lobby, which also contained the statue of a young boy holding a copper umbrella.

Architectural Details of Movie Palaces

The Uptown's foyer was inlaid with a series of fabulous two-by-two-inch tiles. The swastika, which became the symbol of Nazi Germany fifteen years after the theater opened, was actually taken from hieroglyphics found in the tombs of ancient Egypt. Photo by Larry Widen

The Oriental (1927)

One of few theaters in the nation decorated in East Indian decor, the Oriental held six gilded life-sized seated Buddhas. A light inside the figures' turbaned heads illuminated a jeweled crown in red and the slits of the eyes in green.

The Oriental Theater boasted eight porcelain lions, glazed in black and metallic gold, as well as nearly one hundred depictions of elephants. Photo by Larry Widen

This cast-iron exit sign was salvaged from the doomed Egyptian Theater in the 1980s.
Photo by Larry Widen

The Egyptian Theater on North Teutonia Avenue, inspired by archaeologist Howard Carter's recent excavation of King Tutankhamen's tomb, opened in December 1926. Local architects Peacock and Frank envisioned that the theater would emulate a pharaoh's courtyard. Six eighteen-foot-tall figures of simulated gold flanked the auditorium to represent the Colossi of Osiris, found in an Egyptian temple built around 1516 BC. In addition, the designers incorporated a multitude of scarabs, golden wings, sun disks, and other mythological symbols of ancient Egypt into the theater's elaborate interior. The lounge furnishings were specially designed replicas of early Egyptian pieces, and even the lighting fixtures incorporated the motif, with cobra patterns used as wall brackets. They paid attention to the smallest details and included pharaoh heads on the cast-iron seat standards visible on the aisles.

The Venetian, at Thirty-seventh and Center Streets, was a 1,500-seat auditorium that replicated an Italian garden complete with flowers, trees, and shrubbery. An intricate electrical system operated thousands of dimmers and bulbs to reproduce the effect of gentle moonlight. Heavy blue-and-wine-colored draperies hung on walls adorned with gold leaf. Two stairways ascended to the mezzanine, where a beautiful promenade led to smoking lounges and restrooms. The exterior of the theater was done in buff-colored terra cotta and red brick. At each corner, a spiral molding of terra cotta was complemented by a large crown of designs that recalled the splendor of the palazzos of Venice. The theater cost more than $500,000 to construct and was created by Peacock and Frank several months after completion of the Egyptian.

The Avalon Theater is a good example of an avid exhibitor's dedication to his business. The theater opened in May 1929 and was three hard years in the making. Milwaukee exhibitor Jack Silliman had drawn up plans in 1926 for an apartment/ storefront complex that would also house his dream theater. After construction had begun on the lot at 2473 South Kinnickinnic Avenue, Silliman ran out of money, and work on the building stopped in 1927. The steel skeleton stood idle for nearly two years while Silliman sought additional financing. Combining any and all building materials available, the theater was built with cinder block, cream city brick, clay brick, and poured concrete. Despite Silliman's efforts to cut costs, he had spent more than one million dollars by the time the Avalon finally opened in 1929. The theater was a mix of architectural styles and included a Mediterranean courtyard, Spanish roof tiling, and stucco walls. Twisted columns, common to Italian architecture, were topped off with Moorish capitals similar to those in Spain's Alhambra and Alcazar palaces.

Architect Russell Barr Williamson also incorporated a blend of hanging lanterns, a proscenium arch that represented Mediterranean acanthus leaves, and two statues of the goddess Athena, patroness of wisdom, arts, and civilization, near the organ lofts. Thanks to the delay, the Avalon also had the distinction of being the first Milwaukee theater that opened with the capability to show the new synchronized sound pictures that were becoming popular since their inception in 1927. Talking pictures had originally been considered a fad by most exhibitors. Very few, if any, built theaters equipped with sound systems, and consequently they faced expensive renovations to retrofit their buildings. By 1928, it was obvious to all that the silent picture era was over, and Silliman outfitted his theater accordingly.

A more modest atmospheric theater, the Zenith, was owned by Edward Maertz, who had started in the exhibition business by helping out at the Comfort Theater, owned by his father, Fred. The Comfort was a small neighborhood movie house located at Twenty-fourth and Hopkins Streets, about one block from the future location of the Zenith. The Maertz family was active in the local business community, with interests in banking and retail investments.

In addition to his other business ventures, Fred Maertz had built the Comfort in 1914, after gaining experience as manager of the Paris Theater on Center Street. His sons William and Edward were both involved in the theater business as independent operators, having grown up in the midst of movies. William was an art buyer for Schuster's Department Store, but he managed the Fern Theater on North Third Street and later became owner of the Colonial Theater on Vliet Street. As one of the founders of the Hopkins Savings and Loan Association, Edward was involved in the business transactions of many neighborhood friends and dreamed of building a theater of his own.

By 1925, Edward Maertz had formed the Northwest Amusement Corporation, an organization of area businessmen who would finance construction and operation of the Zenith. The Zenith was a successful family-run theater: Edward was president; his brother John served as director and organizer of the theater project; and cousin Elwood Strande played the Kilgen organ. Maertz's daughter Frances was cashier until 1929, earning five dollars a week, and then daughter Helen cashiered until 1936. When Helen got married, her father hired a Pathé News cameraman to film the ceremony and showed the results during the following week's newsreel presentation. Fox-Wisconsin, a regional offshoot of 20th Century Fox, bought the Zenith from the Northwest Amusement Corporation in 1939, just prior to Edward Maertz's death.

The National Theater, at Twenty-sixth Street and National Avenue, designed in 1928 by the prominent local firm Dick and Bauer, was a replica of an ancient Roman garden. The architects incorporated balconies and ledges covered with foliage, marble pillars, plush draperies, fountains, and statues into the 1,400-seat theater's design.

With the advent of the movie palace in Milwaukee, a tug-of-war between local independent owners and the Hollywood movie studios intensified. With the power from their growing local chain of theaters, Saxe AE was in direct competition with the studios, who wanted a bigger share of the market. Warner Brothers, Fox, and Universal were all attempting to establish guaranteed Milwaukee outlets for their pictures. The majority of local theater owners, who had only limited capital with which to compete, were caught in the middle of this power struggle.

$1,100,000 THEATER'S OPENING CROWD

THRONG at premier of Saxe's New Uptown theater yesterday. More than 2,000 persons jammed the playhouse   which has opened a new development on the northwest side. The new movie house was built at a cost of $1,100,000.

Theater openings were major events in the 1920s. Opening-night seats were in demand, and the shows were regularly sold out. The Uptown opened in 1926.
Larry Widen Collection

The Tower was designed by local architects Dick and Bauer, the same team responsible for the Oriental and many other Saxe theaters.
Photo by Albert Kuhli

To fortify their chain of theaters against outside interests while building up the chain's value for potential future sale, the Saxe brothers quickly opened the Uptown, Plaza, Garfield, Oriental, and Tower Theaters in key neighborhoods around the city.

The Garfield, at Third and Locust Streets, was the most elegant of the five new Saxe theaters, modeled after a Viennese opera house. It was designed by Dick and Bauer, who also created the Tower at Twenty-seventh and Wells Streets and the Oriental on the corner of Farwell and North Avenues. The Tower had a Mediterranean feel and was somewhat of a sister theater to the Oriental, but it was not nearly as lavish.

The Oriental, which opened in July 1927, cost $1.5 million, three times as much as the Tower, and the differences showed. Considered by Saxe AE to be the crown jewel in its empire, the Oriental was touted as the city's "premier movie temple." At

The Majestic, once Milwaukee's most popular theater, closed during the Depression in 1932. As was common in the 1920s, the Majestic showed both live acts and motion pictures.
Dave Prentice Collection

Saxe AE's urging, Dick and Bauer conceived an elaborate and mystical theater that incorporated elements of East Indian, Moorish, Islamic, and Byzantine architecture to create what they called "the most beautiful and artistic temple of Oriental art to be found anywhere in America." Elaborate plasterwork featured more than one hundred elephants, as well as numerous mythological creatures. Huge murals of the Taj Mahal and other exotic structures enhanced the lobby's mystique. Mock teakwood timbers, a trio of eight-foot chandeliers, two thousand yards of silk, and a tiled staircase to the balcony and promenade all added to the wonder of the theater.

Despite the strength of films in the latter part of the 1920s, theaters were still being designed with stages to accommodate live shows as well as motion pictures. The Oriental had a large orchestra pit, six dressing rooms, and a lighting control board that supposedly was equal to that of the Roxy Theater in New York City. Opening night at the Oriental featured a stage show called *Mystic Araby*, with Billy Adair and the Arabian Nights Orchestra. Newsreels, a Felix the Cat cartoon, and an organ recital preceded the feature film, *Naughty but Nice*, with Colleen Moore. The price of admission was forty cents, and the 2,310-seat house was filled to capacity for all three shows.

The Saxe brothers celebrated their twenty-fifth anniversary in the film business in 1927. Six months later, they sold everything to a subsidiary of 20th Century Fox.

Milwaukee Journal

The other Saxe palaces were the Plaza at Thirteenth Street and Oklahoma Avenue and the Uptown at Forty-ninth Street and North Avenue. The Plaza incorporated Gothic styling, and the Uptown was modeled after a Roman villa.

With the success of their theaters, Saxe Amusement Enterprises was a highly sought after commodity. In December 1927, Saxe AE sold all of its theater leases for two million dollars to the Wesco Corporation. Within six months after the sale, Wesco was purchased by the Fox Film Corporation, later known as 20th Century Fox. With its purchase of the Saxe chain, Fox controlled exhibition rights in sixty Wisconsin theaters, more than half of them in Milwaukee.

Three months prior to the Saxe sale, a major upheaval shook the moving picture industry, changing it forever. Talking pictures had arrived.

Although reluctant to face the high cost of remodeling their theaters for sound, owners quickly discovered that people were no longer interested in silent pictures. By 1928, twelve theaters in Milwaukee had been converted to sound, and by 1929, the number had risen to fifty-eight. During the first year of the Depression, twenty-one more theaters installed sound movie equipment. Theaters that did not convert fell by the wayside. The Arcade on North Third Street, Chopin on South Thirteenth Street, Pastime on North Avenue, Silver City Gem on National Avenue, and Venus on Green Bay Avenue were among the theaters that closed for good in 1929.

Despite the closings of a number of neighborhood houses, the late 1920s proved to be a tremendously active construction period for theaters in Milwaukee. A total of sixteen new theaters were built in 1927 alone, representing 18,200 new seats at a cost of seven million dollars. These numbers would never again be equaled. In

Talking Pictures: The Evolution of Sound in Cinema

As early as 1908, theaters advertised "talking pictures." Shows performed at the Grand Theater, later remodeled and renamed the Princess, were typical; a group of actors hid behind a partition and shouted out the appropriate lines in time to the action taking place on the screen. The gimmick proved popular in Milwaukee, and when O. T. Crawford lost the Grand's lease to Saxe AE in 1909, Otto Meister offered the novelty at his Vaudette and Butterfly Theaters.

Efforts to record sound together with film actually began much earlier than in the 1900s, though the technology was not common until early in the twentieth century. While working on his Kinetoscope, Thomas Edison announced that he and his assistant, W. K. L. Dickson, were perfecting "an instrument which would do for the eye what the phonograph does for the ear, and that by the combination of the two, all

motion and sound could be recorded and reproduced simultaneously." Dickson's original experiments filming motion pictures involved using photographic cylinders similar to those cylinders used in Edison's sound-producing Gramophone, with another to record sound in time with the moving images. In December 1889, Dickson played for Edison what may have been the world's first talking motion picture, a short film of Dickson tipping his hat and speaking, and then counting on his fingers to demonstrate that sound and images were recorded at the same time. The result of Edison's labors was the Kinetophone, an apparatus with stethoscope-like tubes that provided a reasonably synchronized, if somewhat squeaky, soundtrack to the Kinetoscope's "peep show" films. At the time, Edison's invention was only mildly received by the public,

(continued on next page)

PROPOSED $750,000 THEATER AS SEEN FROM THE AIR

FOND DU LAC

During the active theater construction period, in 1927, Universal Pictures proposed a large theater, office, and retail complex at Twenty-seventh and Fond du Lac. The project never got off the ground.
Milwaukee Journal

addition, theaters costing another two million dollars were proposed. An example was the Arabia, a 1,500-seat palace that was to be located on North Third Street near Center Street. Although construction had actually begun on the theater, financing fell through and the Arabia never got past being a hole in the ground.

During the building boom of the late 1920s, owners also raised the seating capacity of theaters, especially the downtown houses. For example, in 1910 the average capacity for a downtown picture theater was three hundred. By 1920, the average house seated twelve hundred, and by 1930, the average downtown picture palace had two thousand seats.

In 1928, Radio Keith Orpheum (RKO), owners of the Palace Theater on Wisconsin Avenue, hired Kirchhoff and Rose to design the Riverside Theater just six blocks east. Done in the French baroque style, the Riverside featured bronze doors, marble walls and floors, gold-leaf trim, and plush wall draperies. The 2,558-seat auditorium was an elegant study in antique ivory, gold, and peacock blue tones. Five

Talking Pictures: The Evolution of Sound in Cinema

(continued from page 77)
many of whom were leery of spending too much time in the darkened penny arcades.

Other attempts to link sound and film included the Photocinemaphone (1906) and the Cameraphone (1910). Tom Saxe installed the latter in the Lyric Theater as a Milwaukee first. Still other methods such as the New Kinetophone (1913), Webb's Electric Pictures (1914), the Photokinema (1921), and Phonofilm (1923) came and went as scientists searched for a workable method of capturing and amplifying sound. Most early attempts to capture sound with film involved a wax disk synchronized with a movie camera, but this method had numerous drawbacks, including poor audio quality and very short recording times, forcing directors to limit scenes to ten minutes. Throughout the 1920s, however, several companies developed means of capturing sound directly on the film, which eliminated the difficulty of aligning sound with the images.

It was not until 1926, with the development of the Movietone and Vitaphone systems, that sound became an integral part of the cinematic experience. In Milwaukee, the first talking picture, *When a Man Loves*, played at the Garden on Wisconsin Avenue in September 1927. In October, Warner Brothers unveiled *The Jazz Singer*, with a talking and singing Al Jolson. The movie industry changed overnight. Milwaukee theaters were soon playing pictures billed as "All Laff —All Talk," letting people know at a glance that a particular theater had the newest rage in movies.

Oddly enough, movie studio executives were reluctant to adopt the new technology. In an era when studios often owned the theaters that showed movies they made, executives did not welcome the expense involved in outfitting sometimes hundreds of theaters across the country to accommodate the new technology. Additionally, the cost of producing sound films was much greater than it was for silent films, as primitive recording technology sometimes made it necessary to have several cameras running to capture a scene effectively. Another concern was that films shot in English would have a limited market and international revenues would fall. This fear was realized to some extent, but once audiences saw films like *The Jazz Singer* and experienced "talkies," there was no going back to silent film. Despite initial reservations, sound was here to stay.

GARDEN—NOW!
AL JOLSON
in
"THE JAZZ SINGER"
with
VITAPHONE
The GREATEST STORY EVER TOLD
Prices for This Production—
Mats. (to 5 p. m.), 50c;
Eves., Sundays and Holidays, 75c.

The advent of "talking" pictures spelled the end for silent films with organ accompaniment. Theaters built prior to 1927 needed immediate retrofitting to accommodate audio equipment. *Milwaukee Sentinel*

Left: The Riverside Theater was the last of three vaudeville houses in Milwaukee operated by the Orpheum circuit. Orpheum acts first played the Majestic beginning in 1908 and later the Palace at Sixth and Wisconsin. In 1928, the circuit opened the Riverside to present vaudeville shows as well as motion pictures. WHS Image ID 6945

Far left: RKO's Milwaukee venue the Riverside was able to book live superstar performances followed by a film. In its heyday, the Riverside stage was graced by Gene Krupa, Abbott and Costello, Lucy and Desi, George Burns, Jack Benny, and a host of others.
Larry Widen Collection

grand chandeliers sparkled like diamond brooches, complementing thousands of amber, blue, and red lightbulbs that indirectly lit the interior with subdued highlights. A gold-painted domed ceiling loomed high overhead housing the main chandelier.

Below, vaudeville's greatest stars performed on the stage. Burns and Allen, Red Skelton, Jack Benny, Abbott and Costello, and Gene Autry all polished their acts at the Riverside Theater. In later years, Burt Lancaster, Robert Mitchum, Benny Goodman, Gene Krupa, Glenn Miller, and Lucille Ball and Desi Arnaz were among the many stars who appeared there. Although the theater was primarily built for vaudeville, movies were shown from the beginning, usually as support for the starring act. On April 28, 1928, Ezra Buzzington's Rustic Revelers and a Chester Conklin film, *The Big Noise*, headlined the grand opening of the Riverside.

In 1931, as if to defy the Depression that gripped America's purse strings, the grandest of Milwaukee's movie palaces, the Warner, opened on the site previously occupied by the Butterfly Theater. Opening night at the $2.5 million Warner Theater was an extravagant, sold-out affair attended by thousands. Milwaukee photographer Albert Kuhli was hired by Warner Brothers to photograph the inaugural festivities. Kuhli

(continued on page 82)

Celebrities in Milwaukee

Beginning even before the heyday of film, a surprisingly large number of entertainers have had ties to the Milwaukee area. Stage performers from Milwaukee include turn-of-the-century escape artist Harry Houdini, nightclub entertainer Hildegarde, and keyboard king Liberace.

Houdini, born Ehrich Weiss in 1874, lived in Milwaukee for part of his youth. Houdini was a shoeshine boy and newspaper vendor when his father took him to see a magician at Jacob Litt's Grand Avenue Dime Museum on Wisconsin Avenue in 1885. The show inspired Houdini to follow a similar career path, and the eleven-year-old left his family in Milwaukee to strike out on his own.

Hildegarde, an early cabaret singer, was born Loretta Sell in 1906 and lived at Fifty-fourth and Vliet Streets. As a teenager, Hildegarde accompanied silent films on the piano in the Lyric Theater down the street from her home. She then majored in music at Marquette University before becoming the quintessential symbol of New York nightlife in the 1940s and 1950s.

Perhaps the most flamboyant personality to emerge from Wisconsin, Wladziu Valentino Liberace was a child prodigy whose musical talents were nurtured by his parents at an early age. Lessons at the family home at Forty-ninth Street and National Avenue were quickly supplanted by a full scholarship to study piano at the Wisconsin College of Music on Prospect Avenue. By the time he was fourteen, Walter, as he now called himself, made his professional debut as

Before they became movie stars, many familiar names endured the hardships of the road as vaudeville attractions performing live on Milwaukee's theater stages. Mae West was just one. *Milwaukee Sentinel*

a soloist with the Chicago Symphony. In 1940, the twenty-one-year-old, now simply known as Liberace, was a star attraction at the Plaza Hotel in New York City. His long career playing nightclubs, concert halls, motion pictures, and Las Vegas spectaculars was still ahead of him.

Milwaukee was also home to Alfred Lunt, who ruled the Broadway stage for nearly half a century with his wife, Lynn Fontanne. Born in 1892, he lived in a grand mansion on the southwest corner of Seventeenth Street and Wisconsin Avenue until his father's death. Then eight-year-old Alfred found comfort by attending plays at the Pabst, Bijou, Alhambra, and Davidson Theaters—an early influence that led him all the way to the bright lights of New York.

Stage performers weren't the only stars with ties to Milwaukee. Beginning in the early twentieth century, silent film stars like Mae West, Roscoe "Fatty" Arbuckle, and Theda Bara took the spotlight, and all had important events take place in Milwaukee. West's is an intriguing bit of silent film trivia. While on tour in Milwaukee in April 1911, she married her vaudeville partner, Frank Wallace. Etta Wood, an older cast member on the bill, had convinced the seventeen-year-old West that her promiscuity would eventually get her in trouble. She said, "Listen, Mae, with all these men tomcatting around, sooner or later something's going to happen to you. Marry Wallace and be respectable."

Onetime silent movie king Fatty Arbuckle's career foundered after he was accused of murdering party

Celebrities in Milwaukee

girl Virginia Rappe. Even though Arbuckle was acquitted, his public deserted him. After a stage show in 1925 at the Strand Theater on Wisconsin Avenue, police were called to restrain women's groups, concerned citizens, and members of the clergy who were protesting the disgraced comedian's appearance there.

Silent film star Theodosia Burr Goodman, who lived in Milwaukee as a teenager, was the daughter of a Jewish tailor from Cincinnati who brought the family to Milwaukee around 1895. Goodman longed to be an actress, and the suggestive dances and racy dialogue she delivered from the stage of Schlitz's Alhambra Theater shocked more than a few patrons. Goodman left Milwaukee in 1903 and soon found work in motion pictures. Several years later, a public relations flack at 20th Century Fox rearranged the phrase "Arab death" to form the name Theda Bara, and a silent movie star was born.

The technical advancement of sound in cinema produced even more celebrities. Film actor William Joseph Patrick (Pat) O'Brien, born in 1899, lived at Fifteenth and Clybourn Streets. He spent his Tom Sawyer–inspired childhood hopping freight trains in the nearby Menomonee Valley, selling roasted potatoes on Wisconsin Avenue, and playing baseball and football with his friends. His angelic features made him the perfect choice for altar boy in his parish. When O'Brien went to Marquette High School, he met his lifelong friend, Spencer Tracy.

Unlike O'Brien's, Tracy's childhood was troubled. Although his family lived on the elite part of Prospect Avenue, Tracy spent most of his time in the rowdy Irish settlement at Tory Hill, goading boys his age into fistfights. After he set fire to the family home, his parents were able to keep Tracy out of jail only by

Milwaukee's Spencer Tracy (center) in the Howard Hughes film *Sky Devils,* with Ann Dvorak and William Boyd.
WHS Image ID 10990; WCFTR United Artists Still Titles Collection

arranging for him to attend Marquette High School.

When World War I broke out, O'Brien and Tracy immediately joined the navy. Afterward, they decided they could be stage actors and went to New York, where both enrolled at the Academy of Dramatic Arts. Later, as a Warner Brothers film star, O'Brien returned to Milwaukee often in the 1930s and 1940s, making appearances at the Warner Theater on Second and Wisconsin to promote movies such as *Angels with Dirty Faces* and *Knute Rockne—All American*, in which he played along with Ronald Reagan. Spencer Tracy went on to become one of America's best-known film stars, acting in more than seventy-five films over a span of thirty-seven years. Tracy was the first actor to win back-to-back Oscars, for *Captains Courageous* in 1937 and *Boys Town* in 1938.

Above: The elaborate staircase newels in the Warner were made of nickel. This kind of attention to detail is what separated the neighborhood theaters from the downtown palaces.
Photo by Larry Widen

Right: The promenade in the Warner Theater as it appeared on opening night in May 1931. This area became inaccessible to the public when the Warner was changed to a double-screen theater in 1973. Mark Zimmerman Collection

recalled how he was told to "make a lot of noise" and explode flash powder at various intervals, even if he was not really taking a picture, to add to the glamour of the evening.

Newly arriving guests were greeted by forty-four blue-clad ushers who provided curbside service and assistance into the foyer, where a classical string quartet played. The program for the evening began with the "Star Spangled Banner," followed by an address by Mayor Daniel W. Hoan. Next on the bill was a newsreel, two comedy shorts, and a solo performance by Giovanni Martinelli, leading tenor of New York's Metropolitan Opera Company. The evening's feature film was *Sit Tight*, a comedy starring Joe E. Brown. Warner's admission price was the most expensive in Milwaukee: fifty cents for adults on weeknights and Saturdays, sixty cents on Sundays.

The theater was Warner's new flagship in Milwaukee and one of ten theaters under its management there. The others were the Venetian, Egyptian, State, Downer, Kosciuszko, Granada, Riviera, Juneau, and Lake.

The 2,500-seat Warner was designed by Rapp and Rapp and showcased two distinct French architectural styles. The lobby was a three-story exercise in art deco. Huge mirrors, a vaulted ceiling, silver plasterwork, marble veneer, chrome grillwork,

(continued on page 87)

The Projectionists: Putting the Show in Show Business

As late as 1988, Milwaukee's theaters were staffed by projectionists from the Motion Picture Projectionists Union Local 164, an organization that was formed shortly after the first nickelodeons opened their doors. In those days, projectionists hand-cranked the projection machine, and because there were no take-up reels, the film emptied into a canvas sack. In 1909, Edward Medower was working twelve hours a day for fifteen dollars a week in nickel shows on the south side. He started Local 164 that year with three colleagues. The movie industry prospered, and the union quickly gained strength through its affiliations with the International Alliance of Theatrical Stagehands and Employees and with the American Federation of Labor. Until the formation of the Independent Motion Picture Operators Union 110 in 1930 (see the sidebar "The Theater Union War") any projectionist who wanted to work in Milwaukee had to be a card-carrying member of Local 164.

(continued on next page)

A rare glimpse into the projection booth at the Towne Theater in the late 1940s. R. F. Hildebrand

The Projectionists: Putting the Show in Show Business

(continued from page 83)

Gaining admittance to Local 164 was almost impossible unless you were the son or close relative of a member in good standing. Fathers taught sons the business of projecting motion pictures during an initial period of apprenticeship. Then the novice, sometimes called a "stooge," was sent out to several different theaters to perfect his craft under other seasoned veterans. He stopped being a stooge when he was awarded the highest accolade: a union card. Robert Medower, son of Edward Medower and himself a union projectionist for forty-two years, got into the business in 1941 when his father trained him at the Oriental.

A projectionist's greatest concern was the ever-present potential hazard of fire, due to the volatile nature of the nitrate film stock used in moviemaking. If the film broke and got stuck in the gate, it would burn under the intense heat, emitting highly toxic fumes. There were a number of fires in Milwaukee's projection booths over the years, the last one in the Tosa in 1954.

Ambitious projectionists aspired to work in the high-paying downtown theaters. Positions in the deluxe sub-runs (theaters showing films other than first-runs), such as the Garfield or Modjeska, were also highly sought after. Class 5 theaters were "nabes"

(short for neighborhood) like the Pearl or the Kino. Karl Fergens, a projectionist from 1931 to 1978, cited carelessness and apathy as reasons projectionists didn't get the higher positions. "Some of the guys made reel changeovers whenever they wanted, instead of waiting for the cues," Fergens said. At one point during an Esther Williams picture, the star dived from a cliff into the water. A careless reel change might

Don Goeldner, who eventually became a projectionist, visited his grandfather in the Garfield projection booth in the 1960s. Don Goeldner Collection

mean the audience would see her on top of the cliff one minute, and in the water the next.

Longtime projectionist William Dombrock remembered "railroading" film reels between theaters. If the Juneau, on the south side, shared the same film booking with the Century, on the north side, the managers

THE PROJECTIONISTS: PUTTING THE SHOW IN SHOW BUSINESS

would confer about their showtimes, staggering them by about an hour. Then a courier would take three reels that had just played at the Century down to the Juneau, where they would immediately be shown and returned to the Century. Meanwhile, the next three reels, which had just finished showing at the Century, were en route to the Juneau. This cycle went on all day. "That made for a pretty hectic shift," said Dombrock in an interview. "You just crossed your fingers and hoped that the next set of reels got to you in time." Robert Rothschild, an usher at the Layton Park Theater in 1936, railroaded films for years between the Grace and the Layton, the Riviera and the Airway, and the Grand and the Peerless. Rothschild remembered the easiest projection booth to bring reels into was the

Times, because the Trans-Lux projection system was located behind the screen. The hardest booths to get to were those at the Modjeska and Juneau Theaters, each about six flights up.

Most of the older projectionists foresaw the time when there would be no need for a skilled technician in the projection booth. New xenon bulbs, with no open electrical arcing and thus less chance of fire, allowed theaters to get rid of the old carbon arc projectors, which were touchy, finicky pieces of equipment. Once theater made the switch to new projection systems, they could rely on less-skilled labor. The Mill Road triplex was the first theater in the city to switch over in 1970. Today's projection booths are completely automated, and the start of the film is activated by a timer.

The Riviera at Tenth and Lincoln opened in 1921. Photo by Roman Kwasniewski; UWM Archives, Golda Meir Library

The Theater Union War

On a Saturday evening in October 1932, an explosion ripped through the Parkway Theater in Milwaukee, injuring six patrons and causing a mass exodus from the crowded auditorium. The attack drew outrage from citizens, who called for police to end the terrorism that had plagued the city's motion picture houses for the previous two years.

For projectionists who didn't carry cards for Union Local 164, gaining upper-tier jobs in Milwaukee's theaters was difficult, if not impossible. Beginning in 1930, a group of theater projectionists banded together as the Independent Motion Picture Operators Union 110, in opposition to the already established Motion Picture Operators Union 164. The rival unions went to war, with members of each union attacking theaters that hired projectionists from the other. Over the next twenty-four months, chemical bombs, commonly referred to as stench bombs, were detonated in nearly fifty Milwaukee theaters. The Wisconsin, Avalon, Columbia, Granada, Mirth, and Park were among the houses in which shows were disrupted and patrons evacuated because of the noxious fumes. Several chemistry students at Boy's Technical High School were arrested for manufacturing the bombs and in some cases placing them in the theaters.

In addition to the bombings, each of the rival organizations used intimidation and strong-arm tactics as part of their efforts to prevail over the other. Theater managers were threatened, and in several cases assaulted, as the battle escalated. The unions' war reached epic proportions with the Parkway explosion because significant amounts of dynamite and blasting caps were used to create the blast. In an effort to clear its name, Union 164 offered a $3,500 reward for information leading to the arrest of the perpetrators. The Motion Picture Theater Owners of Wisconsin

The Columbia Theater was one of several targets of bombings in the 1930s—the result of a dispute between rival projectionist unions. Larry Widen Collection

convened to discuss closing the Milwaukee theaters until the violence could be stopped. Newspaper editorials asked the theater owners to refrain from closing theaters and instead called for police officials to bring the guilty parties to justice.

On October 28, 1932, Milwaukee police announced the capture of thirty-four-year-old Leslie Jacques and his brother, John. The Jacques brothers eventually confessed to purchasing the explosives from the Waukesha Sand and Gravel Company.

The two unions were eventually able to come together, but they faced the issue of higher pay, which went unresolved until August 1933, when the projectionists threatened to go on strike. At the eleventh hour, an agreement was reached with the theater owners that raised the projectionists' pay from $50 per week to $77.70.

murals, and enormous frosted glass chandeliers made the Warner lobby a breath-taking space to enter. With the mirrors reflecting the chandeliers, grand staircase, and silver ceilings, the area seemed twice as large as it was.

Decorative touches in the hallways deviated from the art deco style to prepare the patron for the elegance of the auditorium. These included draperies and tapestries on the walls as backdrops for period furniture from late-nineteenth-century mansions. Alcoves featured marble statues, fish ponds, and drinking fountains of glazed terra cotta. The auditorium was a complete contrast to the art deco lobby, relying on the French Renaissance style for its quiet splendor. Murals on the upper walls depicted scenes of the eighteenth-century aristocracy and were draped in velvet and lit, along with the rest of the space, by two thousand lightbulbs. Rear walls were covered with rich fabric that was interwoven with gold thread.

Gilbert Freundl, a motion picture projectionist who was employed at nearly all of Milwaukee's theaters in his fifty-year career, remembered the significance of being asked to work at the Warner, downtown's most prestigious house. Freundl said, "When you worked at the Warner, you weren't allowed to make mistakes. They expected the best." Freundl said no one just walked in and started there. "You learned your craft in one of Warner's smaller houses, like the State, or the Downer, out in the neighborhoods, and slowly worked your way to downtown. You had to prove yourself before working there."

The opening of the Warner also marked the beginning of the end of theater building in Milwaukee. Although the Tosa and Times Theaters opened in 1931 and 1935, respectively, the Great Depression effectively ended Milwaukee's seven-year theater construction boom.

FIVE

THE MOVIES PROSPER:
1932–1947

"Thank you for your coffee, seignor. I shall miss that when we leave Casablanca."—*Ilsa Lund (Ingrid Bergman),* Casablanca

Although money was tight for many people in the 1930s, movie attendance stayed strong. The studios experienced some cash problems, mainly because they had millions invested in theaters across the country, along with high-priced talent. But patrons needed a chance to escape the hardships of the Great Depression, and movies served that purpose. Theaters also capitalized on people's financial problems by offering weekly giveaways and hosting games with money prizes, both of which gave moviegoers a sense that they weren't really spending any money to attend the theater. In Milwaukee there would be no fewer than seventy-nine theaters operating simultaneously throughout the 1930s and 1940s.

Typically a neighborhood theater changed its entire program two or three times a week. Without television at home, it was not uncommon for people to go to the theater every time there was a program change. Frances Maertz said that as the Zenith's cashier, she quickly got to know everyone in her neighborhood.

Weekly promotions boosted attendance, especially on slower weekday evenings throughout the 1930s and 1940s. These efforts increased the perception of the movies' value at a time when disposable income was scarce. Theater operators across the country instituted giveaways and contests such as Dish Night, Bank Night, and Grocery Night. On Dish Night, any woman buying a ticket would get a plate, coffee cup, dish, or bowl. Larger pieces such as tureens, serving trays, or pitchers cost two admission tickets, requiring an additional visit to the theater. Owners knew a woman would rarely attend the theater alone, so the giveaway incentive gained

Top: In 1933, Wisconsin Avenue was the premier destination for moviegoers who wanted to see the latest releases.
Dave Prentice Collection

Right: Photographs of the city's neighborhood theaters are rare. These theaters provided affordable entertainment and much-appreciated distraction during the Depression and World War II. Pictured here is the Roosevelt, at Fourteenth and North, in 1940. Karl Thiede Collection

The Aragon Theater, on Howell, was one of many to attract moviegoers with special giveaways— in this case, free dinnerware. Karl Thiede Collection

additional purchased admissions. After a few months of collecting, a household could have a complete set of dishware, many made from what is now commonly referred to as Depression glass. Bob Klein, an usher at the Jackson in the 1940s, said at least one customer each night would drop her dish during the film, and when it broke, the audience would applaud.

Bank Night was another successful attraction, even though there were fewer winners. The theater collected tickets each week and drew one on the designated Bank Night, usually a Monday or Tuesday evening. The winner was required to be present to win. If the winner was not present, the theater returned the ticket to the barrel and increased the jackpot. Sometimes five or six months would pass with no winner, and the jackpot could climb as high as one thousand dollars. In another game, winners were allowed to select their prize from a wheel that offered one-dollar, two-dollar, and five-dollar prizes, plus one fifty-dollar prize. The prizes were hidden, so the winner picked one, hoping to hit the fifty-dollar jackpot. If the first winner didn't get the fifty dollars, the emcee would take it off the wheel for the rest of the night. The next week, the jackpot would climb to sixty dollars, then to seventy dollars, and so on until somebody won.

Another new draw to theaters was the concession stand. Since the nickelodeon

Airway employees at the concession stand. *Connie Murphy Collection*

days, sweets shops and ice cream parlors tended to locate themselves in storefronts adjacent to theaters. Business was brisk both before and after shows. But with the release of *Gone with the Wind* in 1939, in a precedent-setting arrangement, all theater owners who wanted to show the film had to sign a contract requiring them to allow sales of Atlanta-based Coca-Cola during intermission. The ability to purchase a Coke in the theater was so popular with movie-goers that many theater owners added a soda stand. Soon ushers were bringing drinks for sale down the aisles on trays. This evolved into the placement of vending stands in the theater's lobby for the sale of popcorn, soft drinks, candy, and even hot dogs. While only a few theaters had installed permanent concession stands in the early 1940s, nearly every theater had one in the prosperous years following World War II. The concession stand would eventually become a necessity, rather than a novelty, as more and more theaters began to rely on it as a source of revenue.

Although selling snacks at theaters was not a controversial gimmick, the gaming attractions conducted by theater owners raised some eyebrows within the industry. This was partly driven by the knowledge that motion pictures were by and large a self-policed industry. After the risqué nature of films in the 1920s led to the formation of a national censor's office, the last thing the theater wanted was more outside interference. At the Allied Theater Owners of Wisconsin's 1938 convention, one of the topics covered by a keynote speaker was the games. "Movie houses have become little better than fairground concessions," warned Charles Pettijohn, general counsel for the Motion Picture Producers and Distributors of America. "Today's theater owners are not tending to business. They are running crap games, bingo, Screen-o and beano to draw customers." Ray Tesch, general counsel for the Milwaukee Independent Theater Protective Association, responded to the charge. "We would like nothing better than a program of movie entertainment of such quality that people would come for the sheer enjoyment of it." Although cash contests proved to be the best drawing card for the theaters during the Depression years, a Wisconsin law passed in the 1940s made them illegal, although giveaways and contests with prizes that did not involve money were allowed to flourish.

With the theaters established and attendance high, even after contests that involved cash payouts were made illegal, film exhibition had evolved into a sophisti-

(continued on page 94)

Theater Life in the Golden Age: Working for the Movie Palaces

Ushers at the city's premier theaters were expected to assist patrons with their coats
and to locate the best remaining seats. Photo by Albert Kuhli

In forty-plus years of working around movies, Truman Schroeder saw the business go from single screens to mega-screen multiplexes. Schroeder's career began in 1938 at the Brin Theater in Menasha. Fresh out of high school, he went to work as a doorman for ten dollars a week. Schroeder worked from 9:00 a.m. until well past midnight, performing various morning chores such as cleaning or repairing seats before putting on a neat, crisp uniform to greet the first audience of the day. Additional duties included dis-

Truman Schroeder, 1938.
Truman Schroeder Collection

tributing show schedules and theater flyers to local restaurants, hotels, bars, and taxicabs. He even delivered schedules door-to-door in residential areas.

Aside from energy and ambition, neat appearance and good manners were probably the most important requirements of an usher or doorman, who had more contact with patrons than any other employee at the theater. Harold Shaffer, who ushered at Saxe's Tower Theater more than seventy years ago, remembered marching in drills on

Theater Life in the Golden Age: Working for the Movie Palaces

the theater's roof to practice good posture and discipline. Shaffer was seventeen when he started at the Tower, and like all new recruits, he learned his craft in the balcony. A position on the main floor was a highly sought-after prize awarded only to ushers who demonstrated the ability to perform under pressure. Shaffer and his colleagues often ushered more than two thousand people to their seats on a Saturday evening. He worked every evening, and longer on weekends, for a salary of six dollars a week.

A 1927 *Milwaukee Journal* article emphasized the demands placed upon the staff of the Saxe AE theaters:

> No attaché of a Saxe theater is permitted to speak to [a] patron except in a low tone of voice, reflecting refinement and culture. An usher, when addressed by a patron, must answer immediately in polite and concise fashion, giving the patron the information or assistance desired. Ushers are graded each week as to deportment, politeness, and neatness. Any usher falling below 70 percent two weeks in succession is immediately replaced from the waiting list. Before a young man is permitted to join the staff of a Saxe theater, he is carefully investigated. He must come from a good family, possess a good education, and show signs of having had good home training.

Former theater man Wally Konrad worked for nothing just to get his foot in the door of a theater. He was truant from school by age ten and did odd jobs at the Strand in Sheboygan. Konrad changed the canopy letters and cleaned the theater in exchange for movie passes and popcorn.

Harry Boesel remembered peddling handbills and flyers for Sheboygan's Aurora Theater when he was

Girls

Attractive, Possessing Charm and Ability to Meet the Public, for Pleasant, Congenial
USHERETTE
and
PERSONNEL WORK
in One of
MILWAUKEE'S FINEST THEATERS.
Splendid opportunity for advancement to junior executive positions.
PALACE THEATER
APPLY 11:30 A. M. TO 5 P. M.

This Palace Theater ad seeking female workers appeared in the *Milwaukee Journal* in the 1940s. *Milwaukee Journal*

fourteen years old. The Aurora was owned by a man confined to a wheelchair, and Boesel soon became doorman and then assistant manager. Thomas Saxe hired Boesel to work at the Orpheum in Kenosha in 1931. Several years later, Boesel arrived in Milwaukee, working the Garfield and later the Tivoli.

Milton Schultz was an artist and carpenter at the Alhambra Theatre, where he was responsible for creating original displays for the theater's exterior. In 1932, Schultz transformed the Alhambra foyer into an Egyptian tomb for the premiere of Universal's *The Mummy*, starring Boris Karloff. He built a life-sized sarcophagus complete with a mummy to adorn the theater box office. After wrapping the mummy in gauze strips, Schultz doused it with kerosene and set it on fire to create an aged look. Universal sent the Alhambra's display for *The Mummy* on subsequent runs around the country. Schultz recalled that many of his design assignments for a lobby or foyer display began with a train ride to Chicago for an advance screening of the

(continued on next page)

THEATER LIFE IN THE GOLDEN AGE: WORKING FOR THE MOVIE PALACES

(continued from page 93)
film. From there he formulated ideas for exploiting the film, incorporating a slogan or tagline from a studio-issued promotion handbook. As intricate and well crafted as these promotional displays were, most had a life of about two weeks before they were torn down and replaced by material for a new film. Because nothing was permitted to be permanently affixed to the Alhambra's all-marble foyer, Schultz's projects had to be freestanding; he faced the challenge of making them aesthetically pleasing as well as architecturally sound.

Towne Theater owner Joe Reynolds's love for the business began in 1927. As a teenager in Chicago, he began in theater as a bill peddler before quickly becoming an usher and then assistant manager. In 1934, Warner Brothers sent Reynolds to Milwaukee to manage the Lake Theater in Bay View. Later, he was promoted to one of Warner's deluxe houses, the Egyptian on Teutonia Avenue. After several years Reynolds also managed the National Theater. In 1942, Warner gained control of several former Saxe theaters and sent Reynolds to the Oriental on Farwell. He was working there when the record-setting blizzard of 1947 virtually shut down the city for several days. The snow piles were so high the staff was able to stand on them to change letters on the canopy overhanging the side-walk. In May 1955, Reynolds accepted an offer to manage the Towne on North Third Street. His duties there included acting as the local press agent when stars came through town on a tour. Reynolds would meet Jayne Mansfield, Bobby Darin, or Charlton Heston at the airport and take them to the newspapers and TV and radio stations. "Heston even went onstage at the Towne one night," Reynolds said. "The audience really got a surprise that night." After the impromptu appearance, the actor wanted to see the new Jack Webb picture playing around the corner at the Warner, and Reynolds slipped him in and out of the alley doors to avoid causing any more pandemonium.

cated business. The conflict between studio-owned and independently owned theaters was still raging decades after Saxe AE sold its theaters to Fox. As early as 1909, the trade publication *Motion Picture World* ran an appeal to the independent owners to join together "in a united effort to save themselves from the impending actions of the motion picture patent companies, just now starting on its [sic] career of monopoly and extortion." The appeal asked independent operators to create a fund for defense against patent companies that were intimidating exhibitors by threatening to close their houses unless those businessmen signed a license agreement to show the chains' films.

By the late 1930s, the Independent Theater Owners Protective Association had formed to provide powerful mutual support against the Hollywood chains that had become so pervasive. Zenith owner Edward Maertz was president of the association's Wisconsin chapter in 1939 when the state legislature tried to assess a $2.50 tax on all motion picture showings. In protest, Maertz addressed a Senate committee in Madison to get the association's objections on record. Although the tax was directed at film distributors, license agreements between distributors and exhibitors stated that any such tax or fee would be paid by the local exhibitor. In his statement, Maertz claimed the tax would unfairly crush the independent theater owner. To bolster his protest, he said:

> Motion pictures furnish wholesome entertainment for the great mass of our citizens, for the thousands of farmers and workers of Wisconsin, at a price within reach of everyone. In fact, motion pictures have been called the "poor man's entertainment." In these times of continued depression, entertainment and relaxation are as necessary to mental well-being as food is necessary to the body.

The work Edward Maertz did on behalf of the independent theater owners was critical to eventually defeating the tax proposal.

Edward Maertz was a prominent banker who started the Hopkins Savings and Loan institutions. He and his brothers owned the Comfort, Zenith, Fern, and Colonial Theaters.
Frances Maertz Collection

Even with the victory regarding the proposed tax, the independent operators, despite their numbers and due to a hierarchical structure established by those most powerful in the industry, had little hope of ever acquiring quality first-run films for their theaters. All of the city's theaters had been broken down into classifications that ranged from first-run houses, showing the newest and best of the studios' output, to twelfth-run houses. With the major studios controlling many of the city's first- and second-run theaters, the independents were forced into showing third- to twelfth-run films. The lowest theaters on the ladder would not receive a picture until ninety-one days after it had premiered in the city. This practice provided cost savings to any customer who was willing to wait two or three months to see a particular film. The ticket price at the lower-ranking sub-run theaters was ten or fifteen cents compared to the downtown ticket prices of fifty or sixty cents.

In their quest to book better films, the independents were often forced to do block booking. This practice, which required a theater to book a block of a studio's offerings even while the films were still in production, would often tie up an exhibitor's schedule for an entire year. By booking large blocks of films from a particular studio, the exhibitor could only hope to get several big attractions mixed in along the way. Sometimes the promise came true; other times it did not. Although block booking was more advantageous to the studio than to the independent exhibitor, it would eventually hurt the big chains in the long run in the form of crippling antitrust suits.

Because the motion picture studios controlled the production, distribution, and exhibition of their own product, a federal decree in 1939 held them in violation of antitrust laws. Although a Supreme Court decision ordered the studios to divest

(continued on page 99)

The Independent Theater Owners

With less capital and smaller box office revenues than the Saxe brothers, no other Milwaukee exhibitor could compete on equal ground with the city's largest independent. Nevertheless, several enterprising individuals were able to carve a comfortable niche for themselves. Charles Trampe, Jack Silliman, Michael Brumm, Otto Meister, George Levine, Ross Baldwin, and Ben Marcus are among the independent operators who wanted to be free of restrictions imposed by the larger theater chains.

The disadvantage of being an independent operator was that, all too often, the national booking power of the larger theater circuits overwhelmed the small theater owner, who had limited operating capital at best. The late Arnold Brumm remembered many occasions when film booking became a problem at his family's Ritz Theater, founded by his father, **MICHAEL BRUMM**. "The buying power of the chains really put the squeeze on the little guys," Brumm said. "And 'block booking,' the packaging of one great picture with twenty lousy ones, hurt us a lot." Studios often came to the independent owners with a year's worth of projected films. To keep a constant flow of films on his screen, the theater owner bought the lot sight unseen, hoping that several films in the package would turn out to be hit attractions. Until block booking was made illegal in 1939, it was an accepted way to do business. "Film salesmen were very aggressive guys," Brumm said. "They would do almost anything to . . . control your screen for fifty-

two weeks at a time." In spite of the hardships connected with being independent, the most determined of the owners found their markets, and their theaters prospered.

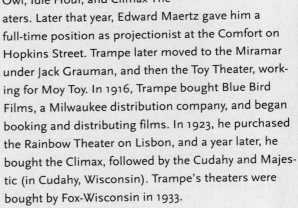

CHARLES TRAMPE was one of these determined owners. A projectionist who made the jump into theater ownership, he joined Local 164, the projectionists' union, in 1913. Trampe was twenty-four years old and served his apprenticeship at the Queen, Owl, Idle Hour, and Climax Theaters. Later that year, Edward Maertz gave him a full-time position as projectionist at the Comfort on Hopkins Street. Trampe later moved to the Miramar under Jack Grauman, and then the Toy Theater, working for Moy Toy. In 1916, Trampe bought Blue Bird Films, a Milwaukee distribution company, and began booking and distributing films. In 1923, he purchased the Rainbow Theater on Lisbon, and a year later, he bought the Climax, followed by the Cudahy and Majestic (in Cudahy, Wisconsin). Trampe's theaters were bought by Fox-Wisconsin in 1933.

One of the first independent operators in Milwaukee to find success on a large scale was **JACK SILLIMAN**, who by the end of the 1920s had amassed a circuit that consisted of eleven theaters. Silliman was born in Lake Mills, Wisconsin, in 1885. He arrived in Milwaukee in 1911 and acquired his first theater, the Liberty, in 1916. In November 1918, he arranged to purchase the lease on the Downer from Oscar Brachman, a powerful real estate broker associated with the Saxe

The Independent Theater Owners

brothers. Brachman also held leases on the Riviera, State, and Kosciuszko Theaters as the agent for owner Mendel Rice. Silliman acquired the leases on these theaters and formed a partnership with theater man Jack Grauman and Arthur Strauss, another influential real estate investor. With Strauss as his backer, Silliman was able to pick up the Juneau Theater from Saxe AE. Shortly afterward, Silliman gained control of the Miramar, Lake, Astor, and Jackson Theaters.

By 1926, Silliman's circuit was successful enough for the owner to consider building theaters of his own. He began with the Venetian on Center Street and planned to erect a similar structure on Kinnickinnic Avenue in Bay View. But even as the Venetian was being constructed, Universal, which already controlled the Alhambra, opened negotiations with Silliman and Strauss to purchase their chain. Silliman, Grauman, and Strauss eventually sold the theater circuit to Universal, who operated the theaters under the name Milwaukee Theater Circuit, Inc.—a monopoly that lasted only until Universal sold the holdings to various bidders, both independent and corporate, in the early 1930s.

While his chain of neighborhood theaters passed from one owner to another, Silliman busied himself with his long-delayed project, the Avalon Theater in Bay View, which finally opened in May 1929. In 1930, Silliman built two Appleton theaters, the Rio and the Appleton. He subsequently sold both houses to the Warner circuit, which retained him as manager. After

Silliman died at his home in June 1942, his wife, Abbie, managed their remaining theaters until her death in 1964.

One of the most colorful of the area's independent owners was **GEORGE LEVINE**. Born in Illinois in 1891, Levine migrated to Milwaukee with Universal Pictures in the 1920s, as head of the company's film exchange. When Carl Laemmle, Universal's founder and president, visited in May 1923, Levine, along with Thomas Saxe, Otto Meister, and other local exhibitors, squired him around town. Levine's favorable position with Universal did not last, however; his career stalled after he backed out of a commitment to marry Laemmle's daughter. Ousted from his post at Universal's Milwaukee branch, Levine purchased the Layton Park, Pearl, and Grace Theaters, operating them under the name LPG Amusement.

Levine had a reputation for being extremely frugal. Rather than buying movie posters from the National Screen Service, he chose to make his own from pressbook clippings. To save carfare, he walked from his Prospect Avenue apartment to the south-side theaters. Levine ran the Grace and Pearl Theaters until 1957, when both closed. He continued to run the Layton Park until 1972, when it was torn down to accommodate construction on South Twenty-seventh Street. Levine died in February 1974.

(continued on next page)

The Independent Theater Owners

(continued from page 97)
ROSS BALDWIN, another independent operator, took a risk when he opened the Wauwatosa Theater at the height of the Depression. Yet, after more than seventy years of continuous operation, Baldwin's "Tosa" Theater (now the Rosebud Cinema Drafthouse) is one of the few survivors of the movie palace era and one of the last remaining single-screen theaters in the area. When it opened on October 22, 1931, admission was twenty-five cents for adults and a dime for children. The Tosa was a family operation for the Baldwins, who lived across the street from the theater. Baldwin was the manager and projectionist until the mid-1930s, when the projectionists' union picketed the theater until Baldwin agreed to hire a union projectionist. His wife, Dorothy, sold tickets. Son Franklyn was the usher, and daughter Jean Mary took tickets at the door. Because of its independent status, the Tosa could not get first-run pictures, but the Baldwins used other methods to increase attendance, including bingo on Tuesdays and giveaways such as cosmetics, pots and pans, flower vases, Bit-o-Honey candy bars, and dish sets. Baldwin also made movies of Wauwatosa residents and events on 16-mm film and showed them at the theater. The hometown films proved to be extremely popular as people returned to see themselves and their friends again and again. Baldwin sold the Tosa Theater to Ben Marcus in 1940.

Unless otherwise noted, all photos are from the Frances Maertz Collection.

The Tosa was one of a handful of motion picture theaters built in the Milwaukee area during the Depression.
Larry Widen Collection

In 1948, the owners of the Towne Theater won a lawsuit against the major film studios to receive first-run status even though it was an independent. This victory for the independent theater owners had long-lasting consequences, allowing the theater to show first-run movies, such as *Breakfast at Tiffany's*, released in 1961.
Joe Reynolds Collection

themselves from the exhibition end of the motion picture business, lengthy litigation held up enforcement of the ruling for another ten years.

In Milwaukee in 1948, a precedent-setting lawsuit against virtually every major film studio was instigated by the independent Towne Theater, owned by Andrew Spheeris and Joe Reynolds. Even though the Towne was one of downtown's largest theaters, it was never able to obtain first-run films because of its independent status. After a long court battle, the U.S. Court of Appeals ruled in favor of the plaintiff, and the Film Board of Trade was ordered to give the Towne first-run status. This hard-fought victory for the independent theater owners came at the height of movie popularity. Theater attendance reached its peak in 1946, with major film studios pumping out films in quantities that would never again be equaled.

Ben Marcus: A Legend in Theater Ownership

The most successful independent theater operator in Wisconsin history was Ben Marcus, who began his circuit with a Ripon theater in 1935. The Marcus family emigrated from Poland in 1925 when Ben was fourteen, settling in Minneapolis. Upon graduation from the University of Minnesota, Marcus took an advertising job with the *Minneapolis Journal*. He started out

Ben Marcus was Wisconsin's most successful independent motion picture operator. The company he founded in the 1930s with one theater now operates more than five hundred screens in four states. Here he is with Jimmy Stewart. Marcus Corporation

selling ads to car dealers and soon moved into the entertainment section. There he began working with the theater owners on their ad copy, and in the process he fell in love with the movie business.

Looking for a theater of his own, Marcus selected a downtown department store in Ripon that was going out of business. For thirty thousand dollars, Marcus purchased the building and remodeled it into the Campus Theater. In the beginning, the twenty-four-year-old showman booked his own films, wrote his own ads, and acted as doorman.

His strategy was simple and effective. By reinvesting all profits directly into the business, he was able to build a statewide circuit of theaters that would eventually dominate the industry. Before long, Marcus owned theaters in Tomah, Sparta, Reedsburg, Oshkosh,

Neenah, and Appleton. In 1940, he acquired the Times and Tosa Theaters in Milwaukee. Two years later, Marcus hired film booker Joe Strother away from Fox-Wisconsin, and shortly afterward, he hired operations manager Henry Tollette. Truman Schroeder joined the company as an usher in 1945.

By the mid-1950s, the Marcus circuit had swelled to twenty-seven theaters, and the company relocated its offices to the seventh floor of the Plankinton Building in Milwaukee. In 1964, Marcus bought several Milwaukee theaters that were once part of the Warner or Fox-Wisconsin circuits, the Warner, Palace, and Telenews. Harry Boesel, longtime manager of the Palace, stayed with Marcus for thirty years after the sale.

Today the Marcus theater group is a powerful chain that still dominates Wisconsin in much the same way that Saxe AE and Fox-Wisconsin once did in Milwaukee and the surrounding area. The Marcus Corporation, run by Ben Marcus's son Stephen H. Marcus, now operates more than five hundred theater screens in Wisconsin, Illinois, Iowa, and Minnesota and owns a number of hotels, motels, and restaurants.

Right: Marcus Theatres began with theaters in smaller Wisconsin towns. By the mid-1960s, Marcus was also in Milwaukee with a circuit that dominated the state much as the Saxe brothers had forty years earlier. *Milwaukee Journal*

During World War II, the theaters' importance as a news source became frighteningly evident when, in 1941, Japan bombed the American naval base at Pearl Harbor. The Avalon and Venetian Theaters interrupted their showings of *Here Comes Mr. Jordan* to announce the disaster. Abbott and Costello's *Hold That Ghost* was halted at the Climax, Zenith, and Tivoli Theaters; at the Granada, *International Squadron*, with Ronald Reagan, was stopped to bring the news to the audience. Later, the Riverside Theater's public-address system played President Roosevelt's declaration of war on Japan to huge crowds on Wisconsin Avenue.

Movie theaters across the nation became powerful venues to financially support the war. Hollywood stars appeared in short films asking members of the audience to buy bonds. One of Milwaukee's most innovative fund-raisers was Arnold Brumm, manager of the Ritz Theater on Villard Avenue. As a child, Brumm did odd jobs at the Princess, a north-side nickelodeon owned by his father, Michael. In summer, when business declined, the Brumm family would travel to outlying areas with a portable generator and a movie projector, bringing the movies to farmers or businesspeople in small towns without movie theaters. The show was done on a weekly circuit, with posters left behind to advertise the next week's feature.

When Michael Brumm opened the Ritz in 1926, he stopped the traveling shows and settled into more routine business operations. Arnold became the assistant manager after graduating high school and eventually took over the business altogether. Although he had always been known for his innovative advertising techniques, such as displaying movie posters upside down, Brumm pulled off his most successful stunt to promote the sale of war bonds in 1944. Coming up short on the bond sales quota set for his theater, Brumm climbed to the top of the Ritz theater's five-story chimney on a Saturday afternoon. A huge sign on the chimney said, "BUY ME DOWN WITH BONDS." He stayed at his post for the next twenty-four hours, and war bond sales were brisk. When the final figures were tallied, Brumm's stunt had doubled the theater's goals.

Harold Fitzgerald's promotions netted millions for the war effort.
Larry Widen Collection

Harold Fitzgerald was another successful war bonds salesman. Born in Milwaukee in 1890, he gravitated toward the theater, obtaining a position with Saxe AE, according to his 1962 obituary in the *Milwaukee Journal*, because of his relationship through an uncle to Thomas Saxe. By the time Saxe AE was sold in 1927 he had gained the post of general manager, second only to the Saxe brothers. He later ran Wisconsin Amusement holdings, where he earned the title "Mr. Movies" during the war years with an impressive record for the sale of war bonds. Fitzgerald originated the slogan "Contribute Your Weight in Scrap" and sponsored innumerable highly successful bond sales stunts.

In the years after World War II, moviegoers turned out to watch Humphrey Bogart, Lauren Bacall, James Stewart, Joan Crawford, Katharine Hepburn, Spencer Tracy, and dozens of other stars, and newsreels continued to supply information about local, national, and world events in America's movie theaters. In 1947, the Telenews Theater opened on Wisconsin Avenue. This unique theater served as a news source, showing newsreels and sponsoring radio broadcasts. A year later, with the advent of television broadcasting, the Telenews began running feature films, although it did install television in its lobby to feature broadcasts from WTMJ, Milwaukee's first TV station. Although television did not at first appear to be a threat to the movies, given its inconsistent picture and high price, its quality soon improved and the price of television sets came down. As more and more families were able to afford televisions, Hollywood's worst nightmare came true: free entertainment in America's living rooms. The movie industry was about to undergo a period of many changes.

The Telenews opened at Third and Wisconsin in 1947 as Milwaukee's first all-news theater. WTMJ television began broadcasting around the same time, and before long the Telenews ceased functioning as a news outlet as more and more homes purchased televisions. Photo by James Murdoch

BRONZEVILLE: A FORGOTTEN LEGACY

FROM THE EARLY 1900s TO THE 1960s, Milwaukee's premiere African American district was known as "Bronzeville." Like Harlem in New York and the Brown Belt in Chicago, Bronzeville was a vital, thriving center of culture for African Americans. Bounded by Meinecke Avenue to the north and Garfield Avenue to the south, Third Street on the east and Seventh Street on the west, Bronzeville shimmered with small businesses, restaurants, and nightclubs owned and operated by blacks. But the biggest business in Bronzeville was music. At the height of the Jazz Age, Cab Calloway, Duke Ellington, Miles Davis, and Lionel Hampton might be found after hours at the Pelican Room or the Moon Glow, "black and tan" nightclubs that welcomed both white and black patrons, a first for the city of Milwaukee. Other forms of entertainment were also popular; over Bronzeville's sixty-year history, ten-cent panoramas at the back of neighborhood drugstores made way for larger movie palaces like the Regal at 704 West Walnut, which offered shows for 25 cents.

In 1960, Bronzeville was forever altered when the city razed part of the neighborhood to make way for the I-43 highway, effectively killing business and forcing mass relocation. The Regal was replaced by a parking lot. Migration of blacks from the South had also flooded the neighborhood job market, and by the 1970s the area was no longer recognizable as the vibrant center it had once been. In 2005, the city of Milwaukee pledged several million dollars to a revitalization project in hopes of resurrecting the legacy of this historic neighborhood.

In the 1940s and 1950s, the Regal was a vital part of the Bronzeville neighborhood's thriving entertainment district.
Wisconsin Black Historical Society

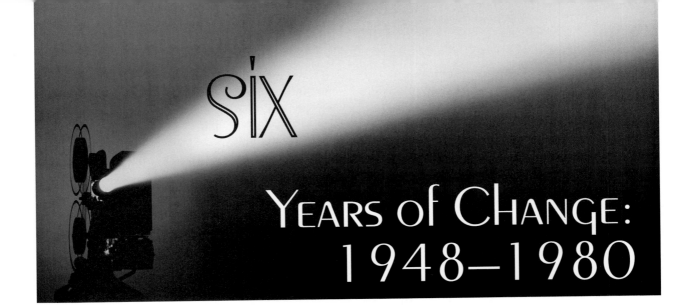

SIX

YEARS of CHANGE:
1948–1980

"A wide screen just makes a bad film twice as bad."—Samuel Goldwyn, 1953

In 1950, there were eighty movie theaters in Milwaukee. Of those, only three—the Airway, Telenews, and Fox Bay—had been built after World War II. By 1960, the number of operating theaters had been reduced by half. There were many reasons for the rapid demise of these theaters, including the population's postwar exodus to newly created suburbs and the availability of television in the city's living rooms.

The main reason for the change was the 1948 antitrust ruling that forced studios to divest their interest in theater chains. The case between Paramount Pictures and the U.S. government, also known as the Hollywood Antitrust Case of 1948, was a touchstone for the movie industry. No longer could studios distribute primarily to the theaters they owned, or to those they had agreements with. Even further, the ruling made ownership of theater chains by studios illegal. Studios like Paramount and Fox were forced to sell their chains, and this, coupled with suburban expansion, had grave implications for the future of the movie house. After the Supreme Court's ruling, routine repairs and remodeling on older theaters stopped abruptly, leaving the buildings to fall into disrepair. And new theaters were built with different aims than the luxury and escapism of the movie palace: convenience and cost-effectiveness drove new theater construction to the suburbs, where population growth showed no sign of slowing in the years following the war. The antitrust case marked the end of the golden age of the movie theater and ushered in what would become the multiplex era, where multiple screens made more showings possible.

The industry was also aware of the threat of television, which boomed in the 1950s. Hedging their bets, some studios sold their library of films to television for

Blockbuster movies like Walt Disney's *Peter Pan*, released in 1953, played to overflow audiences at the downtown theaters.
Milwaukee Journal Sentinel

future broadcasts, further enhancing that medium's growing power. But television, as viewers soon came to find out, didn't have the same production capabilities as the big screen. With longer run times than television shows and larger than life, well-loved film stars topping the bill, there was still a ready audience for film—just less of a desire for the standard plots and stereotyped characters of the Western, the slapstick, and the romance, which took a blow when studios stopped producing large numbers of stock films. To offset the dual impact of television and the antitrust laws, studios began to invest more money in individual films instead of devoting production costs to putting out large numbers of generic—but often forgettable—stock films.

By 1952, the nature of the industry had changed, not least because of a decision made that year by the Supreme Court that protected films from government censorship. The "Miracle Decision," named for the movie that sparked international controversy for its sacrilegious plotline, protected the content of films under the First Amendment. It also cemented the growing consensus that it was film, not television, where "art" was made. But even this did not counteract the loss of numbers at the box office.

As the Hollywood studios' profits eroded, they made a concerted effort to lure people out of their living rooms with gimmicks such as 3-D movies. For a short time, 3-D, a new technique of double projection that produced a three-dimensional image on the screen, had patrons swarming to the theaters. The first feature film

Above: The Fox-Wisconsin chain was the dominant theatrical enterprise in Wisconsin until the early 1950s. With the advent of television, Fox Theaters either closed or were sold to independent showmen. *Milwaukee Journal*

Right: Clever theater owners devised a way to get kids out of the house and into the theaters while Mom prepared Thanksgiving dinner. *Milwaukee Journal*

released in 3-D, 1953's *Bwana Devil*, played in Milwaukee simultaneously at two downtown theaters, the Palace and the Wisconsin, directly across the street from each other. The waiting lines ran around the block at each theater. The popularity of 3-D was short-lived, however, as people soon tired of the novelty—as well as of the headaches and nausea that were caused by careless projection.

Studios also tried to attract audiences with genuine improvements, such as wide-screen Cinerama and CinemaScope, which were much more successful attempts to combat television. The anamorphic lens used to create Cinerama's breathtaking wide-screen images was actually developed in France in 1930. Because it required a multiple-camera and -projector system to create the effect, the Hollywood moguls didn't see much value in using it. But the advent of free entertainment right in the home twenty years later caused Hollywood to reconsider. In 1952, MGM's Louis B. Mayer produced *This Is Cinerama*, a feature-length travelogue that set the movie business on fire. Although extremely expensive to make, the New York opening of the film generated a great deal of interest, and people lined up around the block to see a wide-screen film with multichannel directional sound.

Cinerama was a breath of fresh air. It offered sights and sounds that no television could reproduce. Now Hollywood needed a practical and economic version of Cinerama, and Darryl F. Zanuck, head of 20th Century Fox, acquired the rights to it, renaming it CinemaScope. Fox immediately put two CinemaScope features into production for 1953: *How to Marry a Millionaire,* with Lauren Bacall and Marilyn Monroe, and *The Robe*, starring Richard Burton, Jean Simmons, and Victor Mature. The first cinemas to be equipped with the new screens, lenses, and stereophonic sound systems saw their box office takings skyrocket. Within a few short months, all the major studios had anamorphic features in production, with the exception of Paramount.

Cinerama and CinemaScope films required Milwaukee's downtown theater owners to remodel their auditoriums to accommodate the wider image. Projection booths needed alteration as well to accept the multidirectional projectors. Although alteration costs were initially high, the investments paid off as these special attractions often played for months at a single location on Wisconsin Avenue. The Strand actually sold advance reserved seat tickets for films such as *South Pacific*, *Ben-Hur*, *The Sound of Music*, and *Around the World in 80 Days*. To allow smaller neighborhood theaters to play the new films afterward without any costly renovations, the studios also issued standard flat-screen versions.

One of the most innovative marketers of the era, Walt Disney, embraced the new medium of television and used it to great advantage as he advertised his theatrical releases. The series *The Wonderful World of Disney*, which premiered in 1954, was often little more than a vehicle for Disney to tantalize moviegoers with scenes from the films *Davy Crockett: King of the Wild Frontier*, *Peter Pan*, *20,000 Leagues Under the Sea*, *Old Yeller*, *Pollyanna*, *101 Dalmations*, and *The Absent-Minded Professor*. All were huge box-office successes and demonstrated that television could work in favor of the motion picture studios.

Another improvement—the most important one—was color. Hollywood

Above: Cinerama was one of the techniques that Hollywood employed to compete with television. *Milwaukee Journal*

Right: Overflow crowds wait outside the Towne Theater in 1962.
Joe Reynolds Collection

By 1950s, the Venetian, at Thirty-seventh and Center, had been remodeled into a furniture showroom. By 1989, the Venetian was abandoned and awaiting demolition.
Milwaukee Journal Sentinel

studio heads frantically bought rights to Trucolor, Cinecolor, Technicolor, and other viable color processes as they became available. In the mid-1950s, the new Eastman Color, the precursor to modern color film, was in its final stages of development. Almost immediately, big-budget films on the production slate were shot on color negative film. By the mid-1960s, even low-budget films could utilize color film stock for production. Still, it was only the big-budget films with established stars and first-class production values that really mattered at the box office. Audiences felt epic films like *Ben-Hur* with Charlton Heston or *Cleopatra* with Elizabeth Taylor and Richard Burton simply had to be experienced in a theater.

Despite the success of these efforts, the 1950s proved to be disastrous for some of Milwaukee's exhibitors. The Davidson Theater kept a long-awaited date with the wrecking ball, and the Allis, Grace, Pearl, and Venetian closed.

The Zenith Theater, which closed in 1954, was converted into a church and remains so today. The remodeling was respectful, and a good deal of the theater is still evident. The ornamental fish fountain and starry ceiling have long since disappeared, but the original seats are still intact, as are the proscenium arch and upper organ lofts.

The Department of Theater Inspection concluded that a staggering total of 13,594 theater seats were lost in 1955 and 1956 alone due to closings. By 1960, the Alhambra showed its last films, the low-quality thrillers *H-Men* and *The Woman Eaters.* The sixty-four-year-old theater was torn down soon afterward.

Other downtown theaters, which saw a temporary upswing in attendance from Cinerama and CinemaScope pictures, faced new competition from the recently constructed suburban movie houses. Beginning in the early 1960s, new theaters were built close to shopping malls: Southgate and Point Loomis on the south side, Capitol Court on the northwest side, Mayfair in Wauwatosa, and Ruby Isle in Brookfield. The Mill Road Cinemas, the first triple-screen theater complex in the Midwest, appeared on North Seventy-sixth Street by 1970. The Skyway, originally opened as a twin screen, was remodeled into a triplex by 1973. Similar complexes followed in the Northridge and Southridge Malls. These smaller, architecturally unremarkable auditoriums provided the latest in high-quality projection and sound as well as concession stands that doubled, or even tripled, the size of their predecessors.

The Color Explosion: The Technology That Changed the Face of Film

Color photography was attempted as early as 1861 when Scottish physicist James Maxwell made three photographs of the same object, using green, red, and blue filters. Using a Magic Lantern specially modified with colored filters, Maxwell was able to project the three images simultaneously, reproducing the original colors on a screen. His efforts set the foundation for color photography as well as color cinema, but it was not until 1897 that the first patent for a natural color film process was granted to H. Isensee of Berlin.

"Natural" photographic color systems began to appear at the beginning of the twentieth century. Most early methods of filming in color used an additive process similar to Maxwell's experiment, recording images through red and green, and sometimes blue, screens. From these, the photographer produced a positive strip of film and then projected it using a camera with a revolving screen holding red, green, and blue filters that would add the appropriate color during projection. The system led to a variety of problems, however. Not least of these was the difficulty of capturing three exposures simultaneously. In addition, color cameras and projectors had to run many times faster than black-and-white machines, and they used much longer strips of film. This added physical strain

SHUBERT

ONE WEEK COM. TODAY MAT. MAT., EVERY DAY

The Brilliant Spectacles of the Entire 40 Days of Festivities Attendant Upon the Recent

Coronation of King George V of England

Shown in **Motion Pictures** in All Their Gorgeous Munificence and Natural Colors, Just as They Occurred!

KINEMACOLOR

What the Critics Say:

"Eighth wonder of the world." —Outlook.

"World's Wonder." —N. Y. Times.

"Startling in realism." —N. Y. Herald.

"Wonder worker." —N. Y. World.

"Miracle of the age." —N. Y. Sun.

PRICES

Mat. Daily 2:30 15c and 25c.

Evenings 8:30 15c, 25c, 35c and 50c.

All Seats Reserved

Color film was a novelty employed as early as 1911. The Shubert Theater was quick to capitalize on showing films of King George V's coronation to sellout crowds. *Milwaukee Sentinel*

to the film as well as increasing the expense. What is more, a split second would pass between each of the three exposures, and moving objects were not registered identically, causing the images to be blurred or fringed.

While Maxwell's experiments focused on projection, other techniques altered film after it was shot. Early methods included tinting, toning, hand-coloring, and the Pathé stencil-tinting system. In tinting, a series of frames was colored with dye, and color was often used as a symbolic effect: night scenes were tinted blue, while scenes depicting fire were tinted red. Toning, which was much less common, altered only the black areas on the film. The hand-coloring process, in which artists colored each frame by hand, was much more labor intensive. Another arduous system involved cutting from a strip of positive film areas to be colored in every frame, thus creating a long stencil. In 1905, the Pathé company devised a way to make stencils that could be filled in by separate colors. Once the colors were assigned, the film and stencil were run through a machine that brushed color onto the appropriate frame.

(continued on next page)

The Color Explosion: The Technology That Changed the Face of Film

(continued from page 109)

The advent of sound in the 1920s had a direct effect on early forms of film coloring. The dyes used to tint films made the areas of film where sound was recorded much less responsive, so the sound had to be amplified to a much greater degree. Moreover, sound took movies a step closer to realism, which did not mesh well with the poetic and symbolic uses of color that came from tinting and toning, popular in the 1910s. Sound won out, and color didn't return until "natural" color systems such as Technicolor were made reliable in the 1940s.

In 1922, the Technicolor Corporation unveiled one of the first successful subtractive color systems. A subtractive system created films that did not require a special projector to add color; instead, they worked by filtering portions of a white light source. To accomplish this, photographers made three negatives through red, blue, and green filters. After a positive was made, the film was dyed with that color's complementary color—cyan for red, yellow for blue, and magenta for green—which would absorb or subtract that color during projection. Superimposing the three images resulted in a color image. The first Technicolor camera was a two-color device that recorded green and red light and had noticeably subdued colors. That camera used a prism to split the light after it entered the lens, creating two negatives that were exposed at the same time, without the fringing problem in earlier systems. In the 1930s, Technicolor developed a successful three-color camera that reproduced colors more effectively, leading to more widespread use in the 1930s and 1940s.

Technicolor led the way in color film technology in the 1930s and 1940s and worked diligently to protect its place as the industry leader by investing heavily in research, development, and patents. Research was done with a great deal of secrecy, and very few people working for Technicolor had access to knowledge outside of their particular division. Equipment used for shooting films in Technicolor was rented from the company and could not be purchased. Additionally, film studios wishing to film in Technicolor were required to use the services of a team of Technicolor technicians who gave advice on lighting, makeup, wardrobe, and a host of other studio functions. By the late 1940s, the Technicolor Corporation had a reputation for being difficult to work with, and with the rise of competition, as well as an antitrust suit that the company lost in 1947, Technicolor began to lose its near monopoly in color film.

Ultimately, color films became prevalent in response to television; it was the way to lure people back into the theaters. Color films had been around since the 1920s, but, with the exception of *Gone with the Wind* and *The Wizard of Oz*, studios didn't need to go to that length because moviegoers were content to watch films that were in black and white or strategically tinted to convey a certain mood. In the 1950s, TV put a dent in theater admissions; as a result, color was perfected to make films more competitive.

As shopping mall theaters continued to grow in number, older houses in the city such as the Garfield, Egyptian, Colonial, Century, Liberty, Rainbow, National, and Granada had closed by 1970. The Tower Theater ceased operation in 1975 and was annexed to the former Family Hospital.

In 1979, the Strand was torn down. The Midwest Express Center now occupies

Right: In 1955, the historic Garden Theatre closed its doors permanently. The building originally housed the fabled Schlitz Palm Garden. In 1921, the Palm Garden was converted to a motion picture theater that in 1927 had the distinction of playing Milwaukee's first talking picture.
Karl Thiede Collection

Below: Shopping center theaters continued to increase in popularity as malls became the new main streets. This ad for the Mayfair Theatre at Mayfair Mall appeared in 1965. *Milwaukee Journal*

the site. Later, the Esquire and Towne were demolished to make way for the new federal building plaza. In the summer of 1983, the decaying Apollo Theater at Center Street and Teutonia Avenue was demolished. And in January 1984, the once-mystical Egyptian Theater was condemned and razed.

In August 1984, demolition began on the Princess Theater at 738 North Third Street, the last remaining survivor of the dozen theaters that once existed on Third Street between Wells Street and Wisconsin Avenue. In 1986, the Carpenter Building, which housed the Cinemas 1 and 2, was purchased for demolition. In its final months, the Cinemas operated on a weekend-only basis with horror and action films.

The Warner Theater went through a series of changes before its closing. The owner changed the name to the Centre in 1966 and renovated the theater into a two-screen auditorium in 1973. To coincide with the 1982 opening of the Grand Avenue Mall, the theater was renamed the Grand Cinemas. It closed for good in 1995, the last of the downtown palaces to show films. Today the building's future remains uncertain.

(continued on page 117)

Above: The Atlas Theater, built in 1910 at the corner of Third and North, was remodeled into the Century in 1960. The theater permanently closed six years later. *Milwaukee Journal Sentinel*

Right: The once-popular Egyptian Theater on North Teutonia Avenue closed for good in 1967. The building stood vacant for twenty-five years and was in a state of considerable disrepair when it was torn down. Photo by Larry Widen

Movies Under the Stars: Milwaukee's Drive-Ins

Above: Usherettes greet cars at the Blue Mound Drive-In, circa 1956. Larry Widen Collection

Below: Blue Mound Drive-In ad, 1954. *Milwaukee Sentinel*

of informality." One couple who attended that night turned on their car radio during the newsreel and were impressed that they could "listen to Bob Hope and watch President Roosevelt." Ushers smartly clad in red, white, and blue uniforms directed traffic, while vendors patrolled the aisles selling snacks car-to-car. Simply called the Drive-In at first, the theater changed its name to the Blue Mound Drive-In when competition began to appear.

Drive-ins caught the public's fancy almost immedi-

(continued on next page)

The drive-in theater is an American phenomenon that succeeded because of its ingenious blending of two national passions: cars and movies. The world's first drive-in theater was built in Camden, New Jersey, in June 1933. By 1949, there were more than one thousand drive-ins; by 1958, there were more than four thousand. Today, fewer than nine hundred are in operation. With the closing of the 41 Twin in 2002, the Milwaukee area no longer has any drive-ins.

The first area drive-in opened June 18, 1940, on Bluemound Road in Brookfield. Admission was thirty-five cents per person, and the theater could accommodate about 450 vehicles. The feature program was repeated twice per night, rain or clear. In a review of the opening festivities, the *Milwaukee Journal* noted that women arrived in shorts and slacks, and people smoked, talked, and crunched loudly on snacks such as peanuts. The *Journal* called the drive-in "the acme

Movies Under the Stars: Milwaukee's Drive-Ins

(continued from page 113)

ately, and within ten years of their inception, they were generating more than twenty million dollars a year. They appealed to a different patron at first: the workingman who didn't care to get dressed up, elderly or handicapped people, low-income families, and dating couples. By 1944, drive-in staples included baby bottle warmers, dance platforms, playgrounds, amusement parks, laundry service, dog kennels, picnic areas, barbecue pits, driving ranges, car washes, on-screen bingo, shuffleboard courts, and in-car heaters. The Milwaukee area's second drive-in, the 41 Outdoor, opened in July 1948 on South Twenty-seventh Street in the town of Franklin. The 41 was built by the Standard Theater circuit, whose local holdings included the Bay, Hollywood, and Riverside Theaters. Mayor Frank Zeidler presided at the inaugural ceremonies, cutting the ribbon that let a sellout crowd drive through the gates. The sixty-five-acre complex held one thousand automobiles and boasted a sixty-five-foot-tall screen, approximately nine times the size of an indoor theater screen. Manager Lando Gran said at the time that plans called for a second screen to be added before the end of summer.

Russ Mortensen, who retired as president of Standard Theaters in 1978, said the twin-screen operation was decades ahead of its time. "Multiple screens are commonplace today, but in 1948, it was a new thing," Mortensen said. "Once you did the math, it didn't take much to realize that two screens could be operated for the same price as one." The 41 Outdoor was successful from the start, both because drive-ins were few and far between and because the theater had first-run privileges. When Standard gave up its lease on the Riverside in 1968, the theater's first-run status went to the company's drive-in.

More drive-ins opened in the 1950s, including the 15 Outdoor in New Berlin and the Victory and Starlite in Menomonee Falls. The Starlite was built by Marcus Theatres, which already had nine drive-ins in the state. Hank Tollette, in charge of strategy for Marcus, saw building a theater in Menomonee Falls as an opportunity to stay competitive in the outlying areas while securing extra screens. In 1964, Marcus built the 24 Outdoor in New Berlin. Shortly after, the company took over the operation of the 16 and 57 Outdoor Theaters.

Bob Klein managed the Starlite when it opened on Labor Day weekend, 1955. Klein said the "theater was Marcus's flagship drive-in and had 1,400 auto bays. On opening weekend, admission was eighty-five cents for adults, free for children. Klein said the drive-ins were a great family entertainment deal in those days. He attributed the success of the theater to the size of the older cars, which were bigger and more comfortable than modern

Above: In the 1950s and 1960s, drive-in theaters were often more successful than their traditional counterparts. Patrons could dress casually and eat in their cars, and kids could sleep in the backseats. This ad from the early '60s shows that drive-ins featured many popular films of the day. *Milwaukee Journal*

Movies Under the Stars: Milwaukee's Drive-Ins

Cars line up at the ticket booth at the 41 Outdoor Theater in Franklin. WHS Image ID 26640

automobiles. Families also liked the Ferris wheel, merry-go-round, swing sets, and slides. The Starlite would start showing cartoons around 8:00 p.m. to give everyone time to get back to their cars for the feature.

Truman Schroeder, a regional manager for Marcus

Theatres, recalled that drive-in theaters were a great source of previously untapped revenue for Marcus beginning in 1949. "We opened the 41 Outdoor in Appleton first," Schroeder said. "They were a whole new ball game for us. None of us knew much about

(continued on next page)

(continued from page 115)

As the city's population spread out and rural areas were converted for housing and shopping centers, the large expanse of drive-in theater land became more and move valuable. Drive-ins were sold to developers, and outdoor theaters faced near extinction in the 1990s. The Victory on Lisbon Road was demolished in 1983.
Milwaukee Journal Sentinel

them." Consequently, the Marcus team was unprepared for the onslaught of eager customers who lined up for miles on the highway to get in and who didn't really know where to drive once inside the lot. "The dust they kicked up was incredible," Schroeder said. "All of us, including Ben Marcus, were out on the field parking cars."

The heyday of the drive-in lasted about twenty-five years, and by 1985 many had closed. At one time, drive-ins were on the outskirts of town, but as the area population expanded, so did residential subdivisions. In short, the city caught up to the once-rural theaters. Bruce Olson, president of Marcus Theatres, said many drive-ins, including several run by his company, closed in the 1980s because the land surrounding them became too valuable.

MILWAUKEE AREA DRIVE-INS, 1940–2002

BLUE MOUND DRIVE-IN   **1940–1981**
Opened as the Drive-In
16125 West Bluemound Road
  (Brookfield)

15 OUTDOOR   **1950–1984**
14400 West National Avenue
  (New Berlin)

59 OUTDOOR   **1968–1984**
Highway 59 and County Trunk A
  (Waukesha)

57 OUTDOOR   **1953–1985**
Opened as the Port Outdoor
Highway 57 (Grafton)

41 OUTDOOR   **1948–2002**
7701 South Twenty-seventh Street
  (Franklin)

FRANKLIN 100 OUTDOOR   **1967–1979**
8900 West St. Martin's Road
  (Hales Corners)

16 OUTDOOR   **1960–1972**
Highway 16 (Oconomowoc)

SLINGER OUTDOOR   **1952–1980**
Highway 60 (Slinger)

STARLITE OUTDOOR   **1955–1995**
W124 N8011 Highway 145
  (Menomonee Falls)

24 OUTDOOR   **1964–1994**
13150 Janesville Road (New Berlin)

VICTORY DRIVE-IN   **1950–1980**
N48 W15382 Lisbon Road
  (Menomonee Falls)

The Downer, which opened in 1915, is Milwaukee's oldest continuously operating movie theater.
Larry Widen Collection

The 1930s were peak years for the theater business in Milwaukee, with eighty-nine theaters showing films. Of those, only seven are still in operation: the Downer, Oriental, Tosa (Rosebud Cinema and Drafthouse), Times, Modjeska, Miramar, and Riverside Theaters. The latter three are dedicated to live theater performances rather than movie exhibition. The Downer holds the distinction of being Milwaukee's oldest continuously operating movie theater, having first opened its doors in 1915.

Expeditions through the central city or near south side reveal the vacant lots where theaters once stood and the boarded-up empty hulks that have decayed from the inside out. The Elite, Venetian, Regent, Lincoln, Tower, and Warner sit in once-important business districts, silent testaments to the golden age of movies and the people who brought them to Milwaukee.

Milwaukee's Oriental Theater: A Case Study in Theater Renovation

What happens when a grand old movie palace falls out of step with the times? In many cases, the neighborhoods in which the 1920s-era theaters were located changed over the years, rendering the theater building obsolete. The Egyptian, Apollo, Uptown, Plaza, and countless other Milwaukee movie palaces met the wrecking ball in the decades following the emergence of modern multiplex theaters in suburban commercial zones. Others, such as the Century, Garfield, Tower, and Zenith, fared better. They were successfully renovated into educational centers, hospital annexes, and churches. Some, such as the Venetian and the Warner, are boarded-up old hulks that await whatever fate is in store for them.

Perhaps the most stellar example of a vintage theater still operating in the twenty-first century is the Oriental, at the crossroads of Milwaukee's Farwell and North Avenues. Originally opened in 1927 by Thomas and John Saxe, the theater stayed profitable through the years, unlike most of its cousins. Perhaps the main reason for the Oriental's stability is that after World War II, the neighborhood did not undergo the same kind of transition as the areas surrounding Third and Locust Streets, Capitol Drive and Teutonia Avenue, or Twenty-seventh and Wells Streets, where movie palaces abounded. The post–World War II exodus to newly created suburbs left neighborhoods in a downward economic spiral, and one by one, theaters such as the Burleigh, Roosevelt, Liberty, Violet, Tivoli, Peerless, Rainbow, Regal, and Fern closed down, as did tradesmen, grocers, and other retailers. But the Oriental's east side neighborhood, with its bohemian atmosphere supported in part by University of Wisconsin–Milwaukee students, managed to continue to sustain restaurants, nightclubs, stores, and entertainment venues. The Oriental survived the tele-

The magnificent lobby of the Oriental Theater was a fantasy setting that drew from Far Eastern influences.
Theater Historical Society of America

vision craze of the 1950s and the shopping mall theater mania of the 1960s. Still, by 1972 the theater was starting to show its age. The roof leaked, the old Barton pipe organ was gone, and the beautiful colored lightbulbs that gave the Oriental its mystique had burned out.

Enter Robert, Melvin, and Emmett Pritchett, electricians by trade, who bought the theater in 1972. The Pritchetts cleaned the building thoroughly from top to bottom, replaced nearly one thousand lightbulbs, and installed a new roof. The brothers also put a theater organ, this one a Kimball, back into the auditorium.

Milwaukee's Oriental Theater: A Case Study in Theater Renovation

Overnight, the dusty, tired theater came to life once again. Rock concerts, classic films, midnight movies, comedy shows, and even traveling Broadway plays were welcome at the Oriental. And beginning in 1978, the Oriental stumbled onto *The Rocky Horror Picture Show*, the best piece of good fortune any theater could hope for. The film has been running every Saturday night at Milwaukee's Oriental since then, longer than anywhere else in the world. Audiences never seem to tire of dressing up as their favorite character from the film and shouting out the lines along with the actors.

Despite these successes, the Oriental again faced financial difficulties by the mid-1980s, simply because single-screen theaters were being forced out of existence all across the country by multiplex theaters with a dozen or more screens under one roof. Landmark Theatres, which currently operates the Oriental by lease agreement, decided that turning the eighteen hundred–seat movie palace into three smaller theaters was the only way to keep the doors open. Sensitive to the decor and ambience, the architects and planners were careful to preserve every detail from the original auditorium as they designed two smaller theaters nestled under the balcony. In 1988, the renovated Oriental opened to the public with a gala party and a showing of the 1926 classic silent film *Ben-Hur*. Even cynics agreed that if the theater had to be altered, it had been done in the most tasteful and appealing way.

The Oriental is a delightful, if unique, example of what can be done to preserve an aging theater if all the variables—location, cost, and demand—are taken into account. It is a living museum, providing movie-goers a sense of what it was like to attend a movie in the heyday of Hollywood.

The Oriental (shown here in 1937) has entertained Milwaukee moviegoers for nearly eight decades. In 2005 *Entertainment Weekly* magazine named the Oriental "One of the 10 Best Movie Theatres in America." Photo by Henry Hunter; Courtesy of the Historic Photograph Collection, Milwaukee Public Library

AFTERWORD

THE SHOW MUST GO ON

From a technology standpoint, the 2006 cinema experience is better than ever. Surround sound, first installed in the late 1980s, puts the viewer right at the center of the action. Climate control ensures a comfortable experience no matter what the outside temperature. And theaters are returning to a more luxurious ambience. Stadium-style seating assures a clear view of the screen from anywhere in the house. Padded, reclining seats complete with cup holders make for a relaxing and comfortable experience. At some locations, soda and popcorn are even accompanied by wine and tapas.

But while the operators of today's theaters have certainly moved on from the spartan look and feel of the 1970s multiplexes, they aren't investing in the elegant decor and elaborate chandeliers of the 1920s. For the vast majority of theater owners, renovation is not motivated by a desire to return to the glory days of the movie palace. Instead, it's motivated by competition.

People don't go to the movies as often as they used to. According to the web information service Internet Movie Database Pro, in 2004 Americans spent $8.5 billion on DVD and video rentals and $11 billion in outright purchases. Industry audits show consumers are renting thirty-five million DVDs each week. By contrast, we spent only $9.4 billion on movie tickets, with just five films (*Shrek 2*, *Spider-Man 2*, *The Passion of the Christ*, *The Incredibles*, and *Harry Potter and the Prisoner of Azkaban*) accounting for almost 20 percent of that number. Any theater owner paying attention to these figures will take pains to see that his or her operation is as attractive and appealing as possible. That bodes well for movie fans who aren't content to watch a good film on a television screen, no matter how large.

But another movement is beginning to take root in Milwaukee: a small but growing interest in theater preservation and restoration. In 2005, Milwaukee's Avalon Theater was the latest to undergo feasibility studies concerning a major restoration. The decision to restore an old theater is not one to be taken lightly.

(continued on page 124)

Movie Prices

Attendance at the movies has been down in recent years, and many analysts blame the availability of DVD rentals and cable television for the decline. Others claim movie prices, reaching $8.50 a head in many theaters, are just too high. But since the beginning, when patrons paid five cents for a seat in the nickelodeon, prices have remained proportionately consistent and in line with the cost of living. As with the rest of the economy, ticket prices through the past century have grown slowly but consistently, reflecting the prices of other consumer goods. As inflation in the later part of the twentieth century affected the price of everything from gasoline to a new home, movie tickets kept pace.

In addition to housing the family restaurant, Charles Toy's building on North Second Street was the headquarters for more than a dozen film exchanges and a motion picture theater. *Milwaukee Journal*

In 1904, when the price of a vaudeville show at Milwaukee's Star Theater ranged from ten cents to thirty cents and a good seat at the more "legitimate" Davidson went for two dollars, a nickel movie was the most inexpensive form of entertainment around. When the average worker was earning twenty-two cents an hour, a rocking chair at Boston Store sold for $1.75 and a downtown apartment could be rented for three dollars a week. But a nickel bought a sandwich and beer at a saloon, or a copy of the *Milwaukee Sentinel* and a Hershey bar.

Ten years later, in 1914, movies had become more sophisticated, and five cents was reserved for matinee prices at second-run neighborhood houses. Most ticket prices ranged from ten to fifteen cents, triple the nickelodeon price of only ten years before. A movie ticket was comparable to the cost of two boxes of Jell-O, but it was still less than half the cost of a seat at a Pabst Theater piano concert (fifty cents to $1.50).

By 1928, movie theaters throughout the city had added sound and other luxurious features. The fifteen-cent ticket was a thing of the past. Bargain hunters could take in an "early bird 'til noon" show at one of Saxe's neighborhood theaters for thirty cents, but the evening show at the downtown palaces cost patrons seventy-five cents per ticket. And at the time, customers paid twenty-one cents a gallon for gas to drive to the theater.

During the Depression, money was scarce, and theater owners tried a variety of ways to entice patrons, including lowering ticket prices. The cost of the early bird specials was cut in half, to fifteen cents. Even the elegant Warner found it necessary to offer a twenty-five-cent 'til 6:00 p.m. ticket price. And bargain hunters could stay close to home, paying only ten cents, fifteen cents, or twenty cents to see a movie at their neighborhood theater. Other relief was given in the way of a gas price cut, with drivers now paying as

Movie Prices

In 1941, the State Theater offered features for twenty cents for most shows. Bargain hunters could come out two nights a week for ticket prices of only ten cents. Karl Thiede Collection

little as seventeen cents a gallon during the first few years of the Depression.

As the economy stabilized in the 1940s, '50s, and '60s, so too did the cost of a movie ticket. As the popularity of the downtown theaters began to fade in the late 1960s, they were no longer able to charge premium prices for their seats, and the cost of tickets became more consistent throughout the city. Theaters continued to offer matinees and early bird pricing, but most ticket prices remained around fifty cents throughout the three decades, with some theaters charging as much as two dollars for special shows.

In the last thirty years of the century, new-home costs rose from an average of $15,000 to $145,000.

The average daily newspaper cost increased five times, from ten cents in 1965 to fifty cents in 2004. And a fast-food hamburger, just ten cents in 1970, rose 1,700 percent, to an average price of $1.75, by 2004. Even the cost of a local pay phone call rose by 350 percent, from ten cents to thirty-five cents. Theater ticket prices were not exempt. The fifty-cent ticket price in 1962 rose to close to eight dollars a ticket by 2004. As was the case a century earlier, you can buy yourself a sandwich at a lunch counter for the same price as a movie ticket. With concert tickets topping out at $350 and professional sports venues charging $100 a head for good seats, the movies are the still one of the cheapest forms of entertainment around.

Today, the cost to build a theater like the Avalon from scratch is upwards of $20 million. For a movie palace that cost $1 million to build in 1929, that cost is formidable. The price for a bare-bones restoration of the Avalon is estimated at $500,000; to restore it to its former glory would cost at least ten times that. Yet it appears this venerable Bay View landmark will again entertain as a motion picture theater, largely because of the improvements made to homes and businesses in the surrounding neighborhood. When this occurs, the Avalon will join the ranks of the Oriental, Times, Tosa, Riverside, and Pabst, other Milwaukee theaters that have been given new life in the past few decades.

Preservation efforts are also aimed at keeping theaters that have already undergone restoration up and running. In 1984, the Riverside Theater at Plankinton and Wisconsin Avenues underwent a massive restoration to bring back its original splendor. Housed in the Empire Building and designed by Kirchoff and Rose, the opulent Riverside opened in 1928 as a combination vaudeville stage and motion picture theater. Until the late 1950s the stage hosted live performances by such entertainers as Abbott and Costello, the Three Stooges, Chuck Berry, Judy Garland, Red Skelton, and Frankie Avalon; by the 1970s the Riverside had evolved into a cinema and rock stage, featuring hundreds of popular bands, including Aerosmith, Linda Ronstadt, and Queen. The 1984 restoration kept just one of the original functions of the theater: the projection booth was removed, and the theater was now used primarily for live stage shows. The Riverside's reputation as a popular live-arts venue lasted through the late 1990s, but in the early years of the new millennium the theater started to lose business and even threatened to close its doors for good. In late 2005, Milwaukee businessman and philanthropist Michael Cudahy took over operation of the theater, doing for the Riverside what he had done for the Pabst, which he purchased from the city of Milwaukee a few years before. With the privatizing of ownership, the ailing Pabst was transformed from a liability on the city's books into a highly successful performing arts venue.

Efforts like Cudahy's are at the heart of the theater preservation movement, but it isn't just individuals who are stepping up to the plate. Based outside Chicago, the Theatre Historical Society of America boasts a movie palace museum and an architectural archive. Its vast collection of playbills, posters, business records, and blueprints are helping to preserve the history of hundreds of theaters across the country. The member-driven League of Historic American Theatres, an international preservation society based in Baltimore, is devoted to preserving and rehabilitating the buildings themselves and schedules yearly conferences to promote its cause. The Internet has also become a valuable resource for those interested in theater preservation, not just as a place to bring interested parties together, but as a vehicle for discussion about the plight of older theaters. It's even become a marketplace for buying

The Riverside Theater was restored to its former grandeur in the mid-1980s. Today the theater is a performing arts stage with two thousand seats.
Photo by Larry Widen

and selling endangered properties. Launched in 2000 by filmmaker Patrick Crowley and film historian Ross Melnick, the Cinema Treasures website (www.cinematrea sures.net) is home to hundreds of profiles of aging and forgotten theaters across the country, written by local historians and frequently updated as demolitions—and renovations—are scheduled.

Just as exciting as seeing the vintage theaters rise again is looking ahead to the future of film exhibition. After consulting with architects, projectionists, and other industry experts, the Milwaukee-based Marcus Corporation has created a blueprint for the motion picture theater of the future. In its new theaters, Marcus is taking great care to eliminate difficult viewing angles and extremely wide or narrow

(continued on page 128)

RESTORING THE RIVOLI: A COMMUNITY EFFORT

LOCAL PRESERVATION GROUPS, HISTORICAL SOCIETIES, and community activists are also doing their part to safeguard neighborhood theaters. In early 2006, concerned citizens in Cedarburg, twenty miles north of Milwaukee, made a bold move to protect the town's single-screen Rivoli Theatre. The Cedarburg Landmark Preservation Society had raised enough funds to purchase the theater building, which developers were eyeing as a potential retail space. The CLPS intends to restore the theater to its original 1930s appearance.

The two-story brick building, built in the late 1800s and originally the home of the Boerner Brothers dry goods store, had fallen into disrepair by the time local businessman and former Universal Pictures film salesman Mark Morgan bought it in 1935. With partner Harry Melcher, Morgan spent more than $100,000 to transform the building into a state-of-the-art movie house, with a stunning art deco façade trimmed in chrome, an Electrolite marquee, and a plush interior featuring, according to the opening night program, "the most modern in sound and projection equipment."

The building that houses the Rivoli Theatre in Cedarburg, built in the 1880s, was originally the home of the Boerner Brothers mercantile, specializing in clothing and dry goods. Diane Morgan Collection

Hundreds lined up outside the Rivoli for its grand opening on January 11, 1936, eager to pay twenty-five cents to see the new MGM film *A Tale of Two Cities*. Morgan's wife, Ann Morgan, recalled years later in the Ozaukee County *News Graphic*, "This theater opening in Cedarburg was like an opening on Broadway. I can still remember how beautiful it looked with all those lights."

The Rivoli quickly became a centerpiece of life in Cedarburg. The theater featured first-run films that changed several times a week, Sunday and holiday matinees, and Tuesday bargain nights. Theater manager Morgan also hosted musical performances, talent shows, lectures, church services, and meetings of civic groups in the theater's auditorium.

Morgan and Melcher entered a lease agreement with the Marcus Corporation in 1956. Marcus continues to lease the Rivoli today, offering previously run films at budget prices. Morgan passed away in 1972, and his widow, Ann, sold the building to a local businessman in 1988.

But the Rivoli's roots in Cedarburg run deep. According to the *News Graphic*, the Cedarburg Landmark Preservation Society and the project architects

Restoring the Rivoli: A Community Effort

Above: The Rivoli opened in 1936 in the heart of Cedarburg's lively downtown.
Photo by Guy Brackett; Diane Morgan Collection

Right: As manager and co-owner of the Rivoli for over twenty years, Mark Morgan (seen here in his theater office circa 1939) provided Cedarburg residents with countless hours of entertainment and decades of moviegoing memories.
Diane Morgan Collection

plan to restore the Rivoli's façade and ticket booth, improve the stage, and add dressing rooms. And with plans to host local drama groups and perhaps even film festivals, the CLPS is not simply restoring a building; it is continuing the Rivoli's legacy of community involvement and keeping the curtain up for generations of future moviegoers.

auditoriums. Seat width will increase from nineteen inches to twenty-two inches, and the distance between rows will increase for more leg room. Several screens in the company's newest complex will measure seventy-five feet in width, more than double that of a standard thirty-five-foot screen. And audio quality will be clearer due to technological improvements in the way sound is delivered; uncompressed audio tracks will restore the highest and lowest sound frequencies to the auditoriums' speaker system.

In the next few years most film reels will be replaced by a digital movie image. Much the way theaters built after 1927 were ready to accommodate the new "talking picture" technology, the Marcus Corporation and other theater companies are preparing for the digital revolution and the day in the near future when films will come to their theaters via satellite or cable. These super-sharp digital films will not scratch after repeated showings the way film stock does, and they won't skip or jump because of splices. What's more, the digital film will allow a theater owner to show a film in language other than English or to show a PG-13-rated version of a film in the early evening and an R-rated version later that night.

Changing technology has always had a huge impact on the showing and watching of moving pictures. As the digital "movie palace" of the future becomes a reality, and as the moviegoing public's viewing habits continue to change, we hope this book will help all of us remember—and honor—what came before.

Milwaukee's Movie Theaters

The following is a comprehensive listing of Milwaukee theaters known to have shown motion pictures at some time during their operation. The theaters are cross-indexed by all known names. The original name of the theater contains additional information, such as street address, dates of operation, architects' names (if known), seating capacity, make of organ (if known), and the current status of the building. A superscript number following a theater name indicates that it was the second, third, or fourth theater to use that name. Sources used to compile this list include the *Milwaukee Journal*, *Milwaukee Sentinel*, and *Wisconsin Evening News* daily newspapers; Milwaukee city directories; Milwaukee telephone books; and city of Milwaukee building inspector reports.

Photos of Milwaukee's neighborhood theater fronts are extremely rare. Many of the ones that appear here are courtesy of former theater manager Karl Thiede, who saved the photographs from destruction in the late 1960s.

Karl Thiede Collection

Abby *(See Greenfield)*
2212 West Greenfield Avenue

Academy of Music
(Imperial, Lyceum, Shubert)
623 North Milwaukee Street
1866–1923
Architect: Edward Townsend Mix
Seating: 1,680
Razed

Ace *(See National)*
905 South Fifth Street

Aetna *(See Royal)*
3000 North Twelfth Street

Airdome *(See Union Electric)*
2161 South Kinnickinnic Avenue

Airdome[2]
1502 South Second Street
1911–1912
Razed

Airway
4001 South Howell
    Avenue
1949–1967
Architect: Myles
Belongia
Seating: 550
Razed

Alamo *(See Idle
    Hour)*
1037 South
Sixteenth Street

Alhambra
334 West Wisconsin
    Avenue
1896–1960
Architect: Charles
    Kirchhoff
Seating: 2,500
Organ: 2/6 Wur-
    litzer
Razed

Allis
7224 West Greenfield Avenue
1912–1952
Architect: John Ganser
Seating: 850
Organ: Barton
Retail space

American
742 North Third Street
1910–1924
Architects: Kirchhoff and Rose
Seating: 700
Razed

American[2] *(See Iris)*
2459 West Fond du Lac Avenue

Apollo
2754 North Teutonia Avenue
1911–1921
Razed

Apollo[2] *(See Milwaukee)*
2754 North Teutonia Avenue

Arabia
2700 North Third Street
1926
Architects: Wolff and Ramsthall
Seating: 1,600
Began construction; never
    completed

Aragon *(See Avenue)*
2311 South Howell Avenue

Arcade
North Third Street
1914–1929
Architect: Peter Christiansen

Dave Prentice Collection

Seating: 697
Razed

Armory Hall
(*Imperial*[2])
2674 North Richards Street
1910–1913
Seating: 683
Razed

Astor
1696 North Astor Street
1914–1952
Architect: Hugo Miller
Seating: 752
Retail space

Atlantic
(*See White House*)
739 North Third Street

Atlas
(*Century*)
2342 North Third Street
1910–1966
Seating: 890
Razed

Aurora
3002 North Third Street
1911–1920
Architect: John Roth Jr.
Seating: 598
Office building

Avalon
(*Garden*[3])
2473 South Kinnickinnic Avenue
1929–2004
Architect: Russell Barr Williamson
Seating: 1,637
Organ: 3/8 Barton
Undergoing restoration

Avenue
(*Aragon, Pix*)
2311 South Howell Avenue
1910–1961
Architect: Stanley Kadow
Seating: 481
Razed

Badger (*See Union Electric*)
2161 South Kinnickinnic
    Avenue

Bay (*See Lake*)
2893 South Delaware Avenue

Bell
(*Iris*[2], *Lyceum*[2], *Roosevelt*)
1402 West North Avenue
1911–1965
Architect: Jacob Jacobi
Seating: 797
Retail space

Bergmann
926 Milwaukee Avenue
1911–1915
Seating: 150
Retail space

Bijou
(*Garrick*[2], *Gayety*[2])
631 North Second Street
1890–1931
Architect: Oscar Cobb
Seating: 1,800
Razed

Boulevard
(*Layton, Layton Park*)
2275 South Layton Boulevard
1911–1971
Seating: 600
Organ: 2/5 Barton
Razed

Burleigh
925 West Burleigh Street
1915–1957
Architect: Arthur Swager
Seating: 828
Organ: 2/6 Barton
Church

Butterfly
1212 West Wisconsin Avenue
1911–1930
Architect: August Willmanns
Seating: 1,500
Organ: 3 manual, make unknown
Razed (to make way for the Warner
    in 1930)

Cameo (*See Community*)
6416 West Greenfield Avenue

Connie Murphy Collection

Larry Widen Collection

Capitol
7239 West Greenfield Avenue
1923–1967
Architect: Robert Messmer
Seating: 750
Organ: Kilgen
Office building

Capitol² *(See Milwaukee)*
2754 North Teutonia Avenue

Casino *(See Olympic)*
704 West Walnut Street

Castle *(See Iris)*
2459 West Fond du Lac Avenue

Central
(Delta, Eighth Street Theater, Midge, Nowosci, Pola Negri, Popularity, Pulaski)
1662 South Eighth Street
1910–1953
Architect: Stanley Kadow
Seating: 250
Offices/flats

Centre *(See Warner)*
212 West Wisconsin Avenue

Century *(See Atlas)*
2342 North Third Street

Chopin
(Eagle², Eighth Avenue Theater)
2922 South Thirteenth Street
1916–1929
Seating: 483
Retail space

Cinemas 1 and 2 *(See Wisconsin)*
530 West Wisconsin Avenue

Climax
1954 West Fond du Lac Avenue
1911–1957
Architects: Duggan and Huff
Seating: 1,000
Organ: 2 manual Barton
Razed

Club *(See Empress¹)*
746–756 North Plankinton Avenue

Coliseum
(Cudahy, Empire², White House³)
4763 South Packard Avenue
1909–1963
Seating: 400
Razed

Colonial
(Palace², Player)
1023 Milwaukee Avenue
1910–1914
Seating: 450
Razed

Colonial[2]
7214 West Greenfield Avenue
1910–1912
Seating: 600
Razed

Colonial[3]
1514 West Vliet Street
1914–1926
Architects: Kirchhoff and Rose
Seating: 800
(Remodeled into Colonial[4])

Colonial[4]
1514 West Vliet Street
1926–1964
Architects: Dick and Bauer
Seating: 1,500
Organ: 3/10 Barton
Razed

Columbia (See North Side Turn Hall)
1025 West Walnut Street

Comet
3324 West North Avenue
1910–1956
Seating: 642
Razed

Comfort
2440 West Hopkins Street
1914–1934
Seating: 600
Tavern

Comique
2246 South Kinnickinnic Avenue
1905–1909
Architect: Nicholas Dornbach
Seating: 200
Retail space

Community
(Cameo)
6416 West Greenfield Avenue
1916–1927
Architect: Charles Lesser
Seating: 600
Tavern

Coronet (See Hollywood)
3832 North Green Bay Avenue

Cozy (See Vaudette[2])
1036 East Brady Street

Cozy[2] (See Wauwatosa Theater Delight)
7208 West State Street

Crown
2514 North Teutonia Avenue
1909–1911
Seating: 200
Razed

Crystal
726 North Second Street
1903–1907
Architects: Leiser and Holst
(Remodeled into Crystal[2])

Crystal[2]
726 North Second Street
1907–1929

Architects: Kirchhoff and Rose
Seating: 1,032
Razed

Cudahy (See Coliseum)
4763 South Packard Avenue

Davidson
625 North Third Street
1890–1954
Architects: Burnham and Root
Seating: 1,200
Razed

Delta (See Central)
1662 South Eighth Street

Downer
2589 North Downer Avenue
1915–Present
Architect: Martin Tullgren
Seating: 940
Organ: 2/8 Wurlitzer
Motion picture theater

Larry Widen Collection

Karl Thiede Collection

Eagle
1546 North Twelfth Street
1909–1912
Architect: Charles Lesser
Seating: 209
Razed

Eagle[2] *(See Chopin)*
2922 South Thirteenth Street

East *(See Murray)*
2342 North Murray Avenue

Egyptian
3719 North Teutonia Avenue
1927–1967
Architects: Peacock and Frank
Seating: 1,856
Organ: 2/8 Barton
Razed

Eight Street Theater
(See Central)
1662 South Eighth Street

Eighth Avenue Theater
(See Chopin)
2922 South Thirteenth Street

Electric Joy
1117 Milwaukee
    Avenue
1907–1908
Seating: 400
Tavern

Elite
(Roxy, Mars)
3240 North Green
    Bay Avenue
1910–1952
Architect: Edward
    Kozick
Seating: 700
Warehouse

Embassy
(See Empress)
748 North Plank-
    inton Avenue

Empire
(Granada)
1125 West Mitchell Street
1906–1968
Architect: Anton Dohmen (1906);
    Bakes and Uthus (1927 as Granada)
Seating: 900

Organ: 2/7 Barton
Razed

Empire[2] *(See Coliseum)*
4763 South Packard Avenue
Organ: Kimball

Emporium
(Imperial 5¢ Theater)
626 West Mitchell Street
1906–1908
Seating: 175
Razed

Empress
(Club, Embassy)
748 North Plankinton Avenue
1910–1929
Seating: 1,100
Razed

Empress[2]
(See New Star)
755 North Third Street

Esquire *(See Telenews)*
310 West Wisconsin Avenue

Fern
2556 North Third Street
1911–1955

Karl Thiede Collection

Architect: Charles Smith
Seating: 580
Church

Fond Du Lac Electric *(See Trinz Electric Theater²)*
1465 West Fond du Lac Avenue

Fox Bay
334 East Silver Spring Drive
1950–Present

Architects: Ebling, Plunkett, and
  Keymar
Seating: 916
Motion picture theater

Franklin *(See Lexington)*
1706 West Center Street

Garden
(Little, Newsreel)
235 West Wisconsin Avenue

1921–1955
Architects: Kirchhoff and Rose
Seating: 1,250
Organ: 2/9 Wurlitzer
Razed

Garden² *(See Rialto²)*
1005 Milwaukee Avenue

Garden³ *(See Avalon)*
2473 South Kinnickinnic Avenue

Garfield: Don Goeldner Collection

Garfield
2933 North Third Street
1927–1965
Architects: Dick and Bauer
Seating: 1,800
Organ: 3/11 Barton
Church

Garrick *(See Star)*
612 North Plankinton Avenue

Garrick[2] *(See Bijou)*
631 North Second Street

Gayety *(See Star)*
612 North Plankinton Avenue

Gayety[2] *(See Bijou)*
631 North Second Street

Gayety[3] *(See New Star)*
755 North Third Street

Gem
(Home[2]*)*
931 South Fifth Street
1909–1938
Architect: Charles Lesser
Seating: 320
Razed

Gem[2] *(See Lyric*[2]*)*
923 Milwaukee Avenue

German Kino *(See Iris)*
2459 West Fond du Lac Avenue

Globe
1220 West Walnut Street
1907–1917
Architect: John Menge Jr.
Seating: 468
Vacant

Goldstein Theater *(See Scenes of the World)*
184 West Wisconsin Avenue
1902–1904
Seating: 50
Razed

Grace
3303 West National Avenue
1911–1957
Architect: Henry Hansel
Seating: 644
Organ: 2 manual Barton
Vacant

Granada
(See Empire)
1125 West Mitchell Street

Grand
738 North Third Street
1904–1909
Architect: John Menge Jr.
Seating: 800
(Remodeled into Princess)

Grand[2]
2917 North Holton Street
1911–1975
Architect: John Roth Jr.
Seating: 790
Church

Wally Konrad Collection

Greendale Historical Society

Grand[3]
(Iris[3]*)*
1125 Milwaukee Avenue
1914–1954
Seating: 950
Industrial space

Grand[4] *(See Warner)*
212 West Wisconsin Avenue

Greendale
5639 Broad Street
1950–1968
Seating: 600
Retail space

Greenfield
(Abby, Pastime[2]*)*
2212 West Greenfield
   Avenue
1913–1957
Architect: Arthur Kienappel
Seating: 530
Meeting hall

H.S. Miller
2200 North Twelfth Street
1909–1910
Seating: 250
Razed

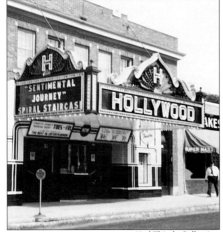

Karl Thiede Collection

Happy Hour
1814 Muskego Avenue
1910–1924
Seating: 590
Razed

Hollywood
(Coronet)
3832 North Green Bay Avenue
1924–1959
Architect: John Bruecker
Organ: 2 manual Barton

Home *(See Trowbridge)*
2827 West Clybourn Street

Home[2] *(See Gem)*
931 South Fifth Street

Ideal *(See Trinz Electric Theater*[2]*)*
1465 West Fond du Lac Avenue

Ideal[2] *(See Vaudette*[2]*)*
1036 East Brady Street

Idle Hour
(Alamo)
1037 South Sixteenth Street
1911–1954
Architect: Name illegible on permit
Seating: 680
Organ: 2 manual Barton
Retail space

Imperial *(See Academy of Music)*
623 North Milwaukee Street

Imperial[2] *(See Armory Hall)*
2674 North Richards Street

Imperial[3] *(See Toy)*
720 North Second Street

Imperial 5¢ Theater
(See Emporium)
626 West Mitchell Street

Iola Electric
1023 North Eleventh Street
1907–1908
Seating: 175
Razed

Iris
(American[2]*, Castle, German Kino, Radio, Show)*
2459 West Fond du Lac Avenue
1911–1966
Architect: Charles Lesser
Seating: 838
Razed

Iris[2] *(See Bell)*
1402 West North Avenue

Iris[5] *(See Grand*[3]*)*
1125 Milwaukee Avenue

Jackson
1322 North Jackson Street
1915–1956
Architects: Van Ryn and
    De Gellecke
Seating: 834
Razed

Juneau
609 West Mitchell Street
1910–1965
Architect: Henry Hengels
Seating: 1,097
Organ: 2/5 Wurlitzer
Retail/office space

Kosciuszko
1337 West Lincoln Avenue
1915–1943
Architect: Arthur Swager
Seating: 735
Razed

Lake
(Bay)
2893 South Delaware Avenue
1926–1956
Architects: Peacock and Frank
Seating: 970
Commercial/residential space

Layton/Layton Park
(See Boulevard)
2275 South Layton Boulevard

Legion *(See Wright)*
734 East Wright Street

GENE AUTRY in MELODY RANCH and SANDY GETS HER MAN and STOOGES

Liberty: Karl Thiede Collection

Lexington *(See Franklin)*
1706 West Center Street
1911–1961
Architect: Gustave Dick
Seating: 548
Organ: Schuelke 1 manual tubular
    pneumatic
Razed

Liberty
2623 West Vliet Street
1911–1966
Architect: Henry Hengels
Seating: 493
Organ: 2/5 Barton
Razed

Lincoln
1104 West Lincoln Avenue
1910–1955
Architect: Stanley Kadow
Seating: 490
Organ: 2/3 Barton
Vacant

Lisbon
(Royal²)
2428 West Lisbon Avenue
1910–1920
Architect: Henry Hengels

Seating: 500
Organ: Barton
Razed

Little *(See Garden)*
632 North Third Street
(Entrance formerly at 235 West
    Wisconsin Avenue)

Locust *(See Pulaski²)*
821 East Locust Street

Lorraine *(See Owl)*
1932 West Fond du Lac Avenue

Lyceum *(See Academy of Music)*
623 North Milwaukee Street

Lyceum² *(See Bell)*
1402 West North Avenue

Lyric
311 West Wisconsin Avenue
1908–1913
Architects: Ferry and Clas
Seating: 250
Razed

Lyric² *(Gem²)*
923 Milwaukee Avenue
1909–1911
Seating: 188
Retail space

Lyric³
3804 West Vliet Street
1917–1952

Karl Thiede Collection

Architect: John Menge Jr.
Seating: 575
Retail space

Magnet *(See Vaudette)*
735 North Third Street

Majestic
219 West Wisconsin Avenue
1908–1932
Architects: Kirchhoff and
  Rose
Seating: 1,902
Condominiums

Majestic[2]
(Oakland[2]*)*
4768 South Packard
  Avenue
1910–1933
Seating: 500
Organ: 2/8 Barton
Razed

Majestic[3]
3620 East Layton Avenue
1927–1980
Architect: Myles Belongia
Seating: 742
Medical complex

Mars *(See Elite)*
3240 North Green Bay Avenue

Merrill
211 West Wisconsin Avenue
1915–1930
Architects: Brust and Phillips
Seating: 1,298
Razed

Merrill Park
455 North Thirty-fifth Street
1916–1930
Seating: 450
Razed

Mid City *(See White House)*
739 North Third Street

Midget *(See Central)*
1662 South Eighth Street

Karl Thiede Collection

Miller
(Towne)
717 North Third Street
1917–1979
Architects: Wolff and Ewens
Seating: 1,700
Organ: 2 manual Barton
Razed

Milwaukee
(Apollo[2]*, Capitol*[2]*, National*[4]*, Ritz*[2]*)*
2754 North Teutonia Avenue
1921–1975
Architects: Dick and Bauer
Seating: 1,140
Organ: 2/9 Wurlitzer-Barton
  composite
Razed

Miramar
(Oakland)
2842 North Oakland Avenue
1913–1954
Architect: George Ehlers
Seating: 800
Performing arts theater

Mirth
2651 South Kinnickinnic Avenue
1913–1952
Architect: William Buscher
Seating: 870
Organ: 2/3 Barton
Vacant

Modjeska
1124 West Mitchell Street
1910–1923
Architect: Henry Lotter
Seating: 900
(Razed for Modjeska[2])

Modjeska[2]
1124 West Mitchell Street
1924–Present
Architects: Rapp and Rapp
Seating: 2,000
Organ: Barton 3/10
Performing arts theater

Mojuvate
(White House[2]*)*
1002 Madison Avenue

KINGS ROW
ANN SHERIDAN
BIRTH OF THE BLUES
B CROSBY M MARTIN

BACK THE ATTACK BUY BONDS HERE

Larry Widen Collection

New Star
(Empress[2], Gayety[3], Orpheum[3], Saxe)
755 North Third Street
1906–1955
Architects: Kirchhoff and Rose
Seating: 1,500
Razed

Newsreel *(See Garden)*
632 North Third Street
(Entrance formerly at 235 West
  Wisconsin Avenue)

North Side Turn Hall
(Columbia)
1025 West Walnut Street
1880–1936
Architects: Rau and Kirsch
Seating: 1,600
Razed

Nowosci *(See Central)*
1662 South Eighth Street

1910–1920
Seating: 450
Razed

Mozart
1316 South Sixteenth Street
1910–1952
Architect: Peter Christiansen
Seating: 433
Retail space

Murray
(East)
2342 North Murray Avenue
1911–1952
Architects: Schutz and Seeler
Seating: 638
Organ: 2 manual Barton
Razed

Mystic *(See Wauwatosa Theater
Delight)*
7208 West State Street

National
(Ace, Palace, Palace Pictures)
905 South Fifth Street

1906–1938
Architect: Charles Lesser
Seating: 266
Industrial space

National[2]
1610 West National
  Avenue
1911–1912
Architect: Charles Lesser
Seating: 390
Razed

National[3]
2616 West National
  Avenue
1928–1970
Architects: Dick and
  Bauer
Seating: 1,388
Organ: 3/10 Barton
Razed

National[4] *(See Milwaukee)*
2754 North Teutonia
  Avenue

ADAME LA ZONG
FARGO KID

Mozart: Karl Thiede Collection

Oakland (*See Miramar*)
2842 North Oakland Avenue

Oakland[2] (*See Majestic*[2])
4768 South Packard Avenue

Oasis (*See Savoy*)
2626 West Center Street

Ogden (*See Studio*)
816 East Ogden Avenue

Olympia (*See Trinz Electric Theater*[2])
1465 West Fond du Lac Avenue

Olympic
(*Casino*)
704 West Walnut Street
1909–1917
Architect: John Menge Jr.
Seating: 274
Razed; Rose Theater built on this
site in 1917

Oriental
2230 North Farwell Avenue
1927–Present
Architects: Dick and Bauer
Seating: 2,110
Organ: 3/14 Barton; 3/32 Kimball
since 1990
Motion picture theater

Orpheum (*See Theater Delight*)
203 West Wisconsin Avenue

Orpheum[2] (*See Palace*[3])
535 West Wisconsin Avenue

Orpheum[3] (*See New Star*)
755 North Third Street

Owl
(*Lorraine*)
1932 West Fond du Lac Avenue
1911–1923
Architect: Charles Lesser
Seating: 480
Vacant

Pabst
114 East Wells Street

Larry Widen Collection

1895–Present
Architect: Otto Strack
Seating: 1,750
Organ: Ferrand and Votey
Performing arts theater

Palace (*See National*)
905 South Fifth Street

Palace[2] (*See Colonial*)
1023 Milwaukee Avenue

Palace[3]
(*Orpheum*[2])
535 West Wisconsin Avenue
1915–1974
Architects: Kirchhoff and Rose
Seating: 2,437
Organ: Wangerin
Razed

Palace Pictures (*See National*)
905 South Fifth Street

Paradise (*See Toy*)
720 North Second Street

Paradise[2]
6229 West Greenfield
Avenue
1929–1996
Architect: Urban Peacock
Seating: 1,239
Organ: Barton
Church

Paramount (*See Queen*[2])
3302 West North Avenue

Paris
2202 West Center Street
1911–1930
Architect: Herman Schnetzky
Seating: 520
Church

Park
725 West Mitchell Street
1907–1954
Architect: Henry Lotter
Seating: 405
Retail space

Parkway
(Rock River)
3417 West Lisbon Avenue
1913–1986
Architects: Rosman and Wierdsma
Seating: 994
Organ: 2/9 Moller
Razed

Pastime
(Warren)
2614 West North Avenue
1910–1929
Seating: 593
Razed

Pastime[2] *(See Greenfield)*
2212 West Greenfield Avenue

Pearl
1700 South Nineteenth Street
1917–1957
Architect: Herman
  Buemming
Seating: 660
Organ: 2/5 Barton
Warehouse

Peerless
917 Monroe Avenue
1907–1908
Razed

Peerless[2]
424 East Center Street
1913–1958
Seating: 454
Razed

Penny Arcade *(See Wonderland Scenic)*
739 North Third Street

Pix *(See Avenue)*
2311 South Howell Avenue

Player *(See Colonial)*
1023 Milwaukee Avenue

Plaza
3067 South Thirteenth Street
1927–1959
Architect: Arthur Kienappel
Seating: 1,308
Organ: 2/7 Marr & Colton
Razed

Pola Negri *(See Central)*
1662 South Eighth Street

Popularity *(See Central)*
1662 South Eighth Street

Princess
738 North Third Street
1909–1984
Architect: Henry Lotter
Seating 900
Organ: 2/5 Hinner
Razed

Princess[2]
3531 West Villard Avenue
1912–1925
Seating: 250
Razed

Princess[3] *(See Wauwatosa Theater Delight)*
7208 West State Street

Princess[4]
In North Milwaukee

Pulaski *(See Central)*
1662 South Eighth Street

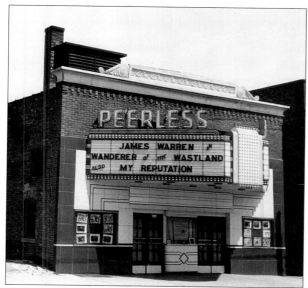
Karl Thiede Collection

Photo by Albert Kuhli

Pulaski[2]
(Locust)
821 Locust Street
1911–1919
Architect: Robert Messmer
Seating: 358
Retail space

Queen[1]
2901 West Clybourn Street

Queen[2]
(Paramount, Tivoli)
3302 West North Avenue
1910–1952
Architect: Charles Lesser
Seating: 500
Community hall

Radio *(See Iris)*
2459 West Fond du Lac Avenue

Rainbow
2718 West Lisbon Avenue
1911–1965
Architect: Wesley Hess
Seating: 603
Razed

Regal *(See Rose)*
704 West Walnut Street

Regent
4011 West North Avenue
1915–1929
Architect: Arthur Swager
Seating: 878
Organ: 2/7 Barton
Vacant

Rex *(See Union Electric)*
2161 South Kinnickinnic
    Avenue

Rex[2]
Fifty-eighth Street at National
    Avenue

Rialto
316 West Wisconsin Avenue
1921–1925
Architects: Kirchhoff and Rose

Karl Thiede Collection

Seating: 834
Razed

Rialto[2]
(Garden[2]*)*
1005 Milwaukee Avenue
1920–1976
Seating: 750
Retail space

Ritz
(Villa)
3610 West Villard Avenue
1926–1995
Seating: 840
Organ: 2/5 Kilgen
Vacant

Ritz[2] *(See Milwaukee)*
2754 North Teutonia Avenue

Riverside
116 West Wisconsin Avenue
1929–Present
Architects: Kirchhoff and Rose
Seating: 2,557
Organ: 3/13 Wurlitzer 235
    Special
Performing arts theater

Riviera
1005 West Lincoln Avenue
1921–1954
Architect: Charles Lesser
Seating: 1,200
Organ: 2/5 Wurlitzer
Warehouse

Rivoli *(See Silver City Gem)*
3506 West National Avenue

Rock River *(See Parkway)*
3417 West Lisbon Avenue

Roosevelt *(See Bell)*
1402 West North Avenue

Rose
(Regal)
Built on site of former
    Olympic/Casino)
704 West Walnut Street
1917–1924 and 1939–1958
Architect: George Zagel
Seating: 500
Razed

Rosebud Cinema Drafthouse
(See Tosa)
6823 West North Avenue

Karl Thiede Collection

Seating: 50
Razed

Schultz Electric Theater
2005 West Vliet Street
1906–1907
Seating: 175
Razed

Sherman
4632 West Burleigh Street
1935–1977
Architect: Herbert Tullgren
Seating: 932
Vacant

Wally Konrad Collection

Roxy *(See Elite)*
3240 North Green Bay Avenue

Royal
(Aetna)
3000 North Twelfth Street
1909–1913
Seating: 244
Razed

Royal[2] *(See Lisbon)*
2428 West Lisbon Avenue

Royal[3] *(See World)*
830 South Sixth Street

Royal[4]
Forest Home Avenue at Eighteenth
  Street

Savoy
(Oasis)
2626 West Center Street
1914–1975
Architect: Martin Tullgren
Seating: 860
Organ: 2 manual Barton
Wisconsin Black Historical Society
  and Museum

Saxe *(See New Star)*
755 North Third Street

Scenes of the World
(Goldstein Theater)
184 West Wisconsin Avenue
1904–1906

Karl Thiede Collection

Shorewood
4329 North Oakland Avenue
1929–1952
Architect: George Zagel
Seating: 1,136
Organ: 2/7 Barton
Razed

Show *(See Iris)*
2459 West Fond du Lac
   Avenue

Shubert *(See Academy of Music)*
623 North Milwaukee Street

Silver City Gem
(Rivoli)
3506 West National Avenue
1911–1929
Architect: Charles Lesser
Seating: 462
Office/warehouse

Star
(Garrick, Gayety)
612 North Plankinton Avenue
1899–1909
Architects: Kirchhoff and
   Rose
Seating: 2,000
Razed

Star[2] *(See Trinz Electric Theater*[2]*)*
1465 West Fond du Lac
   Avenue

State
2616 West State Street
1915–1955
Architect: Frank Andree
Seating: 967
Organ: 2 manual Kimball
Vacant

Strand
510 West Wisconsin Avenue
1914–1978
Architects: Wolff and Ewens
Seating: 2,000

Karl Thiede Collection

Organ: Wangerin-Weickhardt
Razed

Studio
(Ogden)
816 East Ogden Avenue
1926–1965
Seating: 586
Organ: 2/4 Barton
Razed

Syndicate Electric
2480 West Walnut Street
1907–1908
Seating: 250
Vacant

Telenews
(Esquire)
310 West Wisconsin Avenue
1947–1981
Architect: Ralph Phillips
Seating: 471
Razed

Theater Delight
(Orpheum)
203 West Wisconsin Avenue
1907–1913
Seating: 340
Razed

Theatorium
184 West Wisconsin
   Avenue
1906–1923
Seating: 242
Razed

Times
5906 West Vliet Street
1935–Present
Architect: Paul Bennett
Seating: 500
Motion picture theater

Tivoli *(See Queen*[2]*)*
3302 West North Avenue

Tosa
(Rosebud Cinema Drafthouse)
6823 West North Avenue
1931–Present
Architect: Paul Bennett
Seating: 560
Motion picture theater

Tower
757 North Twenty-seventh Street
1926–1975
Architects: Dick and Bauer
Seating: 1,609
Organ: 3/10 Barton
Extended care facility annex

Towne *(See Miller)*
717 North Third Street

Toy
(Imperial[3]*, Paradise)*
720 North Second Street
1915–1924
Architect: Alexander Guth
Seating: 460
Razed

Trinz Electric Theater
1202 West Mitchell Street
1906–1907
Architect: Nicholas Dornbach
Seating: 247
Retail space

Trinz Electric Theater[2]
(Fond du Lac Electric, Ideal, Olympia, Star[2]*)*
1465 West Fond du Lac Avenue
1906–1914
Architect: Nicholas Dornbach
Seating: 300
Razed

Trowbridge
(Home)
2827 West Clybourn Street
1910–1913
Seating: 250
Razed

Union Electric
(Airdome, Badger, Rex)
2161 South Kinnickinnic
    Avenue
1906–1919
Seating: 275
Apartment/ Retail space

Unique
2355 North Third Street
1909–1915
Seating: 188
Razed

Unique[2] *(See Wauwatosa Theater Delight)*
7208 West State Street

Unique Electric
1012 West Mitchell Street
February–April 1907
Seating: 73
Razed

Universal *(See Wagner)*
1636 West Forest Home
    Avenue

Uptown
2323 North Forty-ninth Street
1926–1981
Architects: Rapp and Rapp
Seating: 1,818
Organ: 3/10 Barton
Razed

Varsity
1326 West Wisconsin Avenue
1938–1976
Architects: Grassold and Johnson
Seating: 1,114
Marquette University theater/
    lecture hall

Vaudette
(Magnet)
735 North Third Street
1908–1923
Seating: 492
Razed

Vaudette[2]
(Cozy, Ideal[2]*)*
1036 East Brady Street
1908–1914
Seating: 168
Razed

Venetian
3629 West Center Street

1927–1954
Architects: Peacock and Frank
Seating: 1,430
Organ: 2/8 Wurlitzer
Vacant

Venus
3329 North Green Bay Avenue
1918–1928
Architect: John Bruecker
Seating: 499
Razed

Victoria
1037 West Winnebago Street
1911–1918
Seating: 664
Razed

Villa *(See Ritz)*
3610 West Villard Avenue

Violet
2450 West Vliet Street
1915–1956

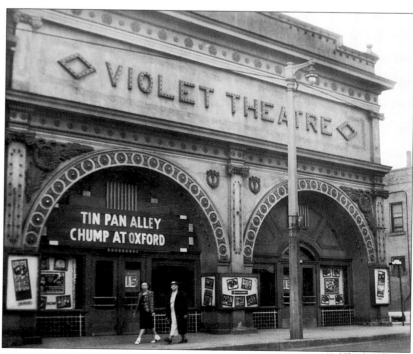

Karl Thiede Collection

Architect: Edward Kozick
Seating: 546
Razed

WAGNER
(Universal)
1636 West Forest Home Avenue
1913–1917
Architects: Herbst and
    Hufschmidt
Seating: 371
Vacant

WARNER *(Centre, Grand[4])*
212 West Wisconsin Avenue
1931–Present
Architects: Rapp and Rapp
Seating: 2,431
Organ: 3/28 Kimball
Vacant

WARREN *(See Pastime)*
2614 West North Avenue

WASHINGTON
3516 West Lisbon Avenue
1911–1923
Architect: Theodore Schutz
Seating: 404
Razed

WAUWATOSA THEATER DELIGHT
(Cozy[2], Mystic, Princess[3], Unique[2])
7208 West State Street
1911–1922
Seating: 400
Tavern

WHITE HOUSE
(Atlantic, Mid City)
739 North Third Street
1916–1955
Architect: Henry Lotter
Seating: 1,365
Organ: Schuelke
Razed

WHITE HOUSE[2] *(See Mojuvate)*
1002 Madison Avenue

WHITE HOUSE[3] *(See Coliseum)*
4763 South Packard Avenue

WISCONSIN
(Cinemas 1 and 2)
530 West Wisconsin Avenue
1924–1986
Architects: Rapp and Rapp
Seating: 3275
Organ: 3/17 Barton
Razed

WONDERLAND SCENIC
(Penny Arcade)
739 North Third Street
1906–1914
Seating: 500
Razed

WORLD
(Royal[3])
830 South Sixth Street
1928–1985
Architects: Gurda and Gurda
Seating: 832
Vacant

WRIGHT
(Legion)
734 East Wright Street
1910–1944
Architect: Henry Hengels
Seating: 414
Community hall

ZENITH
2498 North Hopkins Street
1926–1954
Architects: LaCroix and Memmler
Seating: 1,363
Organ: 2/7 Kilgen
Church

Bibliography

Articles

Bernard, Richard. "Harmful Elements: A History of Censorship in Milwaukee." *Milwaukee Magazine* 9.3 (1984): 51–54, 88.

Conlee, Courtland. "Baghdad in Milwaukee: Recalling the Great Days of Third Street." *Milwaukee History* 3.2 (1980): 38–46.

Gomery, Douglas. "Movie Exhibition in Milwaukee, 1906–1947: A Short History." *Milwaukee History* 2.1 (1979): 8–17.

Gomery, Douglas. "Movie Theater History in Wisconsin." *Marquee* 12.4 (1980).

Gomery, Douglas. "Saxe Amusement Enterprises: The Movies Come to Milwaukee." *Milwaukee History* 2.1 (1979): 18–28.

Gomery, Douglas. "The Warner: Architectural Splendor in Milwaukee." *Marquee* 12.1–2 (1974).

Gurda, John. "In the Light of Liberty: A Fiftieth Anniversary History of the Marcus Corporation." Milwaukee, Wisconsin: Marcus Corporation, 1985.

Headley, Robert. "The Theaters of Milwaukee." *Marquee* (Spring 1971).

Kmet, Jeffery. "Milwaukee's Nickelodeon Era: 1906–1915." *Milwaukee History* 2.1 (1979): 2–7.

Morrison, Craig. "From Nickelodeon to Picture Palace and Back." *Design Quarterly* 93 (1974): 6–17.

Mueller, Theodore. "I Remember When the Movies Were Flickers." *Historical Messenger of the Milwaukee County Historical Society* 23.2 (June 1967): 55–59.

Widen, Larry. "Milwaukee's Dime Museums." *Milwaukee History* 8.1 (Spring 1985): 24–34.

Widen, Larry, "Milwaukee's Princess Theater." *Marquee* (Spring 1985).

Widen, Larry, and Judi Anderson. "When Milwaukee Loved Movie Palaces." *Heritage* 4 (Winter 1984).

Books

Austin, Russell. *The Milwaukee Story*. Milwaukee: The Milwaukee Journal Co., 1946.

Fielding, Raymond, ed. *A Technological History of Motion Pictures and Television*. Berkeley: University of California Press, 1967.

Gardiner, Helen. *Art Through the Ages*. 7th ed. New York: Harcourt Brace Jovanovich, Inc., 1980.

Grau, Robert. *The Business Man in the Amusement World*. New York: Broadway Publishing Co., 1910.

Hall, Ben M. *The Best Remaining Seats*. New York: Clarkson N. Potter, Inc., 1961.

Hartt, Frederick. *History of Italian Renaissance Art*. New Jersey: Prentice-Hall, 1979.

Israel, Paul. *Edison: A Life of Invention*. New York: John Wiley & Sons, 1998.

Lindsay, Vachel. *The Art of the Moving Picture*. New York: Liveright Publishing, 1970.

Naylor, David. *American Picture Palaces*. New York: Van Nostrand Reinhold Co., 1981.

Neale, Steve. *Cinema and Technology: Image, Sounds, Colour*. Bloomington: Indiana University Press, 1985.

Ramsaye, Terry. *A Million and One Nights*. New York: Simon and Schuster, 1926.

Rossell, Deac. *Living Pictures: The Origins of the Movies*. Albany: State University of New York Press, 1998.

Salt, Barry. *Film Style and Technology: History & Analysis*. 2nd ed. London: Starword, 1992.

Sennett, Mack, and Cameron Shipp. *King of Comedy*. Garden City, NY: Doubleday, 1954.

Sexton, R. W., ed. *American Theaters of Today*. New York: Architectural Book Publishing Co., Inc., 1930.

Still, Bayrd. *Milwaukee: The History of a City*. Madison: State Historical Society of Wisconsin, 1948.

Transportation Survey, Milwaukee Metropolitan District. Milwaukee: Mclellan & Junkersfield, Inc., Engineers, 1927.

Correspondence

Lillian Gish, actress, to Larry Widen and Judi Anderson, 1986, authors' collection.

Hildegarde, performer, to Larry Widen and Judi Anderson, 1986, authors' collection.

Claire-Lisette Hubbard, last Princess owner, to Larry Widen and Judi Anderson, 1985, authors' collection.

RKO Distribution Corporation to Michael Brumm, 1943, authors' collection.

Robert Rothschild, retired film distributor, to Larry Widen and Judi Anderson, 1984 to 1986, authors' collection.

Edward Trinz, son of Henry Trinz, to Larry Widen and Judi Anderson, 1986, authors' collection.

INTERVIEWS

Philip Balistreri, former manager of the Princess theater, 1985 with Larry Widen.

William Boehnlein, Thomas Saxe's godson, 1985 and 1986 with Larry Widen.

Harry Boesel, former Fox-Wisconsin and Marcus Theaters manager, 1998 with Larry Widen.

Arnold Brumm, Ritz Theater manager, 1985 and 1986 with Larry Widen.

William Dombrock, retired projectionist, 1992 with Larry Widen.

Cecelia Freuler, John Freuler's niece, 1986 with Larry Widen.

Rudolph Freuler, John Freuler's nephew, 1986 with Larry Widen.

Gilbert Freundl, retired projectionist, 1985 with Larry Widen.

Clem Hinterstocker, former owner of the Miramar Theater, 1985 with Larry Widen.

Claire-Lisette Hubbard, last Princess owner, 1985 with Larry Widen.

Wally Konrad, former theater manager, 1990 with Larry Widen.

Albert Kuhli, photographer, 1984, 1985, and 1986 with Larry Widen.

Frances Maertz, Edward Maertz's daughter, 1985 and 1992 with Larry Widen.

Ben Marcus, founder and chief executive of the Marcus Corporation, 1985 with Larry Widen.

Elmer Nimmer, former manager of the Egyptian, Granada, and Juneau Theaters, 1985 with Larry Widen.

Carlo Petrick, Marcus Corporation, 2006 with Larry Widen.

Walter Plato, retired projectionist, 1992 with Larry Widen.

James H. Rankin, Milwaukee architectural historian, 2005 with Larry Widen.

Robert Rothschild, retired film distributor, 1984, 1985, and 1986 with Larry Widen.

Arnold Saxe, Thomas Saxe's nephew, 1985 with Larry Widen.

Milton Schultz, former theater artist, 1990 with Larry Widen.

Joe Strother, Marcus Corporation executive, 1985 with Larry Widen.

Betty Zagel, Otto Meister's niece, 1985 with Larry Widen.

Frank Zeidler, former mayor of Milwaukee, 1985, 1990, 1998, and 2004 with Larry Widen.

NEWSPAPERS CONSULTED

Evening Wisconsin Milwaukee
Milwaukee Daily Reporter
Milwaukee Free Press
Milwaukee Journal
Milwaukee Journal Sentinel
The Milwaukee Leader
Milwaukee Sentinel

Periodicals consulted

The Billboard
Design Quarterly
Exhibitor's Herald
Historical Messenger
Marquee
Milwaukee Magazine
Milwaukee History
Moving Pictures World
Variety

Web Sites consulted

Cinema Treasures: www.cinematreasures.net
The Internet Movie Database: www.imdb.com
The League of Historic American Theatres: www.lhat.org
Milwaukee Journal Sentinel online: www.jsonline.com
Theatre Historical Society of America: www.historictheatres.org

Miscellaneous

Academy of Music programs. Milwaukee Public Library collection.

Alteration permits, City of Milwaukee Development Center. 809 North Bradley, first floor.

Annual Reports of the Inspector of Buildings. Milwaukee, Wisconsin. 1910–1983.

Avalon Theater programs. Milwaukee Public Library collection.

Bijou Theater programs. Golda Meir Library—University of Wisconsin–Milwaukee.

Building permits, City of Milwaukee Development Center. 809 North Bradley, first floor.

Butterfly Theater handbills. Milwaukee Public Library collection.

Domestic Corporations, 1848–1945, Series 356, Wisconsin Historical Society Archives.

Egyptian Theater programs. Authors' collection.

Garfield Theater programs. Authors' collection.

Majestic Theater programs. Milwaukee Public Library collection.

Meeting minutes of the Board of Directors of Independent Theater Owners of Wisconsin and Upper Michigan. Milwaukee, Wisconsin. 1948. Authors' collection.

Meeting minutes of the Citizens Commission on Motion Pictures. Milwaukee, Wisconsin. 1913–1919. Authors' collection.

Miller Theater handbills. Milwaukee Public Library collection.

Milwaukee Sentinel Amusement Section, *Milwaukee Sentinel*, January 12, 1912.

Milwaukee Sentinel Amusement Section, *Milwaukee Sentinel*, November 13, 1911.

Milwaukee Telephone Directories, 1905–present.

Milwaukee Theater programs. Authors' collection.

Milwaukee Towne Corporation v. Loews, Inc., et al., 190 F.2d 561. United States Court of Appeals Seventh Circuit, July 17, 1951.

Modjeska Theater handbills. Milwaukee Public Library collection.

Once a Year, Milwaukee Press Club, Vol. 20, No. 20, 1914.

Ritz Theater exhibitors' date books, 1928–30, Incorporation Papers of Defunct Domestic Corporations, 1848–1945, Series 356, Wisconsin Historical Society Archives.

Ritz Theater weekly managers' reports, 1932–36, Incorporation Papers of Defunct Domestic Corporations, 1848–1945, Series 356, Wisconsin Historical Society Archives.

Saxe Theater handbills. Milwaukee Public Library collection.

Star Theater handbills. Milwaukee Public Library collection.

Tower Theater handbills. Authors' collection.

Treasures of Tutankhamen. Exhibit. New York: Metropolitan Museum of Art, 1976.

Tribute to John and Thomas Saxe, *Milwaukee Sentinel*, 1939.

Warner Theater programs. Authors' collection.

Wid's Film Daily Yearbooks. Film TV Daily Yearbook of Motion Pictures and Television. New York: Film Daily, 1918–1970.

Wisconsin Motion Picture Industry Reunion and Testimonial, 1938. Milwaukee Public Library.

Wisconsin Theater programs. Mary Granberg collection.

Wright's Milwaukee City Directories. Milwaukee, Wisconsin: "Wright Directory Company." Consulted years 1870–1983.

Zenith Theater programs. Frances Maertz collection.

Usher Harold Schaffer stands fifty feet above the ground on the Tower Theater's vertical sign, 1930. Photo by George Hartwell; Harold Schaffer Collection

Index